Coming to Terms

by

Jon Stamford

Jon Stamford

Jon Stamford was educated at Marlborough College and The University of Bath. After some two decades in academic neuroscience, he was diagnosed with Early Onset Parkinson's Disease in 2006. Jon is a full-time writer-scientist and has published three scientific books. His first non-science book SLICE OF LIFE was recently published. Jon is married with three children.

For a father much loved

and

a mother much missed

Praise for Slice Of Life

I found it very entertaining (I do like the idea of magnetic L plates falling off at 70 mph) and informative (ever since Terry Pratchett mentioned Journey to Samarra in his let's-all-snuff-it lecture I have been wondering what he meant).

Nancy B (columnist)

Seriously good, not that I would have expected anything less. Ok, it had nothing to do with PD but I couldn't help thinking of Hunter Davies' Father's Day column that he used to write in Punch - the antics of members of his family catalogued each month in a witty and erudite way.

Claudia F (freelance writer and editor)

I have been raving about (it) to anyone who would listen since. You accomplish much - science and stories are perfectly intertwined and manage to entertain and inform without being lachrymose. I can't wait for the next installment.

Emma D (editor, social media expert)

(It) has had (us) in stitches, especially the one about the sparkly body glitter!

Zoe M (neuroscientist)

My oldest son, my wife, and I sat around our kitchen table tonight while I read "Christmas Present". We laughed until we cried. I love the phrases such as, "epileptiform abandon", "shaking mouse droppings from my slippers. Thank you for sharing your gift of humor with us this Christmas. I look forward to meeting the ghost of Christmas future.

Bob K (Positively Parkinson's website)

Quite brilliant as you are at writing, I had to down tools for the day. On an afternoon when my artistic flow has completely failed me ....your words have been heartening, provocative and upsetting all at once. I just wanted to say thank you for what you've written.

Nicola H (Interior designer)

Really like this! will add to my favourites

Katie P (Editor of "The Parkinson", PDS magazine)

This is superb ... I really enjoyed reading it and chuckling over it. You certainly have the ability to write an interesting piece.

Veronica E (office administrator)

Hi – loved it! Look forward to the (next) book...

Lyn P (archaeologist)

Great reading! I shall continue to dip in and out

Sara L (teacher)

Love (it). Magnetic ones peel off at 70. Brilliant. Was at a Burns Supper tonight ... with one of my pals who thinks your writing is superb.

Bryn W (Wobblywilliams website)

Acknowledgements

A sense of humour is essential when facing this cruel condition and laughter is the best medicine of all. Scientific studies support this. Really.

This book would not exist without Claire, Catherine, Alice and Alex, who have consistently provided much of the comic source material for this book.

Without their humour and ability to see the funny side of the mundane, there would be no book. There would probably be no author either.

Preface

Parkinson's disease, or *paralysis agitans* as it was first known, is a progressive neurodegenerative condition characterised by tremors, rigidity, slowness of movement and loss of balance.

Every ten minutes of every working day, someone in the UK is diagnosed with Parkinson's, a condition which currently affects more than a hundred thousand UK citizens.

Although Parkinson's is often considered a disease of old age, readers may be surprised to learn that more than one in twenty are diagnosed with the condition before the age of forty.

Despite the nature of the illness, Parkinson's does not kill and symptoms can be ameliorated by drugs, at least in the earlier stages.

Parkinson's is not a death sentence so much as a life sentence.

Further information on Parkinson's and useful websites can be found on the last pages of this book

Newly diagnosed?

It crosses my mind that many of you reading this book may be doing so because you too have been diagnosed with Parkinson's and that you are perhaps looking for guidance or some indication that people can cope, and do cope, with this illness.

I have lived with this now for nearly five years and my best piece of advice to the newly diagnosed would be, in Douglas Adams's words "don't panic". It is possible to live with this condition, and to thrive even. Although Parkinson's will change the things you do, and the way you do them, it will only stop you if you allow it to.

People often react to a diagnosis of Parkinson's in one of two ways. There is the path of destruction, or more accurately self destruction. Don't ask the question "why me?" because it will lead you nowhere. Besides it had to be someone.

Then there is the path of affirmation. Parkinson's will be with you every day and every night. It's an unwelcome houseguest, a squatter even. But until that glorious day when we can evict it from our lives, we would do well to make the best of it.

That's not to say that it's easy. It isn't. It's not say that the path is smooth. Again it isn't. You have Parkinson's, but the Parkinson's does not necessarily have you.

You can be defeated or defined by this condition. Parkinson's can, in so many unexpected ways, give as much as it takes. It's up to you to enjoy those gifts. And you will. Believe me, you will.

Introduction

To write one book (Slice of Life) about the highs and lows of Young Onset Parkinson's Disease can be pardoned as a momentary lapse of judgement, an understandable indulgence on behalf of the writer. Forgiveable and somehow explicable in the context of the illness.

A second book is much less dismissible, and looks to the casual observer like a wholly premeditated and somehow unnecessary act. Readers prepared to tolerate the first volume of rambling indiscretions must surely find their patience tried by a second helping.

And the second book inevitably draws comparisons with the first. Is it as funny as the first? Is there anything left to say? Somehow one feels compelled to try and justify the second volume. It's hard not to be defensive.

If I'm honest I would have to say that I drifted into this second book with the same singular lack of purpose as I had the first. This is just another year in my life. Another ragbag collection of jottings, anecdotes, rants and meanderings on subjects dear and alien to me. I've always enjoyed a good rant.

In the end, I wrote this for no reason other than the fact that large numbers of readers had enjoyed the first, and told me so. If you fall into that group, this book is for you.

Jon Stamford

July 2012

October

It's easy to ignore the satnav. The problem is the little blighter is just too polite. "Turn around when possible" it says. Underneath it thinks "That was the turning you idiot". I imagine it fuming. "I told you in advance ... yes I did ... but would you pay attention? Oh no, too busy eyeing up that dollybird in the Mazda ... don't try to deny it ... I saw you ... too busy to notice the B564 anyway ... don't take that tone with me ... OK, do your own navigation, see if I care ... but don't come crying to me when we're out of petrol in the middle of Dartmoor ... no, don't 'sweetheart' me, I'm not listening ... and you're in the wrong lane ... oh, and that's the oil warning light by the way ... not your day, is it?

THE COWS DOWNSTAIRS
Saturday, 9 October 2010

When I was young, my parents tried to explain, in terms that I might understand, what a 'domesticated' animal was. I have an idea that it related to a piece of homework. For some unfathomable reason, my mother chose to explain it as being 'a bit like living in a house'. I took this literally and applied it as a universal yardstick to man and beast. Grandad Tom for instance was emphatically not domesticated, unless you counted the snug of the Black Bull as a home. Grandad George by comparison was certainly domesticated, subjugated even. The definition worked well enough for people. But try as I did, I couldn't shake off the notion that domesticated animals lived in the house, like some Orwellian tableau. I had visions of pigs enjoying a Sunday lunch in riotous Hogarthian excess, and cattle sleeping on the sofa with today's newspaper.

And the cattle always lived in bungalows. Bet you didn't know this but, because of the way their knees are put together, cows are apparently unable to walk downstairs. Going upstairs is fine but it seems they can't go down stairs, a simple piece of biology that has underpinned many a Cambridge student prank over the years. But next time you go to a department store ask yourself why the leather shoes and handbags are on the first floor. Obvious isn't it. Because they don't want to offend delicate bovine sensibilities. And it clearly works. When did you last meet a Jersey on the stairs? Or see a Holstein standing at customer services to voice a complaint? That's right -- never. Now I think of it, cows are rubbish at escalators and lifts too. So they live in bungalows. Or sheltered housing. And all because of their dodgy knees.

But cows are not the only ones fixated on problems with stairs. Neurologists seem to spend an inordinate amount of time asking whether we, as patients, have trouble with stairs. They wait with pen poised for us to say 'yes' and with a barely suppressed smile tick another box on our impaired quality of living scale. Mind you, answering 'moo' doesn't help either. It took me a good ten minutes to explain about cattle knees and a further ten to make him rub out the tick in the dementia box. No sense of humour some neurologists.

I mention all of this because stairs, on the whole, are okay for us Parkies. In fact they can be a positive help. The most frozen and rigid of us, unable to take a single step on the flat, have no difficulty initiating and continuing movement on stairs, up or down. In fact obstacles generally seem to provide the stimulus we need to lift our feet and start moving. It's called cueing and is one of a bag of party tricks that Parkies adopt to initiate movement. Others I know use music, either real or imagined to get going.

One friend, like me, loved Wagner and used to kickstart himself with the Ride of the Valkyries. Well I say kickstart, but considering he was the size of a Chinook, it was still pitifully slow progress. But once started, you were ill advised to cross his path. Like a supertanker, he was unstoppable. Doubly so in the swimming pool, where the sight of him in Speedos would make grown men blanch. In the end, his knees gave way before his brain, confining him to a wheelchair. Presumably reinforced.

Of course the best way to get a Parkie moving is fear. This was a joke told by Dave Allen some years ago:

It's a miserable winter evening when a drunk leaves the pub and decides to take a shortcut home through the churchyard. There is no moon, it is raining heavily and dark. He fails to see an open grave dug for a funeral the following day, loses his footing and falls in. He picks himself up and tries to get out. But the grave is too deep and the rain has turned the earth into mud. Try as hard as he can, it is too slippery to climb. Eventually he gives up and decides to spend the night there. He curls up at one end of the grave.

A little while later, another drunk leaves the pub and decides to take the same shortcut. Same problem. He too falls into the open grave. The first drunk, still sitting there, listens while the other struggles to escape. This goes on for several minutes. Eventually the first drunk stands, taps the second drunk on the shoulder and says to him "you won't get out". But he did.

Its Latin name is *kinesia paradoxica*. But nobody laughs when I tell jokes in Latin.

CLOCKWISE
Monday, 18 October 2010

When you live with a neurodegenerative condition like Parkinson's, you are acutely aware of the passage of time. As each day ends, you ask yourself 'are we anywhere nearer to a cure?' sometimes aloud, sometimes silently mouthing the words. This is the 'fierce urgency of now'. Because time is important with Parkinson's and the passage of time without change is accusatory. Time should not be wasted and each second should be accounted for. Although not a Parkie, my father would in many respects have made an ideal patient, with his obsession for timekeeping. This fixation with the clock and the passage of time was never more apparent than at holiday time when we might be preparing to go to France for instance.

So obsessive was my father about punctuality that the mere act of going on holiday became an exercise in clock watching. So many potential hazards were envisaged on the road south, so many ways in which the fates might conspire to make us miss the midday ferry to Calais. The journey became Napoleon's retreat from Moscow. Still there was no reason why we should be plucked from our beds at two or three in the morning and piled, sleepy, disorientated and still in our pyjamas, under travel blankets in the back of the car for the long drive to the coast. From Doncaster, the journey was a nominal five hours, six if you allowed for a break. My father, nails gnawed to the quick, and maps akimbo would allow ten.

Even allowing for a fifteen vehicle pileup, a royal funeral cortege, Leeds United returning with the FA Cup, light aircraft landing on the carriageway, or a presidential motorcade, there was no way it would take that long. Allowing for all of them, it still wouldn't take that long.

"We've arrived" my father would say as we drew up in darkness at the quayside. The docks were empty, not another car in sight. And the first person from the ferry company to greet us was a security guard, bewildered by our unexpected appearance. The presence of three children in their pyjamas only further discombobulated him. Bearing in mind that our ferry would not leave for another five hours, his considered opinion -- albeit robustly expressed in the vernacular -- was that our interests would be best served by going somewhere else for four hours until boarding commenced.

Over the course of my childhood, this scene was repeated in one form or another at airports, ports, and stations throughout most of Europe and North America. Often we arrived in sufficient time to catch an earlier departure, and found ourselves bundled hurriedly onto already crowded ferries, trains or aeroplanes, our fastidious punctuality thus managing to achieve the worst of all possible outcomes – a fraught drive followed by a tense hassled flight. Everyone else in the world arrived at the allotted time give or take a few minutes, strolling casually up to the departure gate or stepping onto the train at the last minute, and seemingly none the worse for the experience. But not the Stamfords.

My father was and is always early. Always. And never more so than when he arrived to collect me from university one end of term, knocking on my door with Teutonic precision at exactly ten o'clock on Sunday morning.

His evident delight at his own punctuality was of a magnitude only matched by my surprise at seeing him. He was a week early. Evidently I had failed to establish that he was meant to collect me the following Sunday. Having needlessly driven some two hundred miles, it was, to say the least, an uncomfortable moment. And if that was uncomfortable, it was nothing compared with my stumbling efforts to explain the additional presence of Suzy, who I had met at a party the previous night. I don't suppose it was a million laughs for Suzy either. As I recall she mollified him with pancakes.

I've probably made more of this than I should. I love my father dearly and he knows it. I visit most Tuesdays for a bit of supper and, even with such a loose arrangement, he frets if I am late. We eat paella or lasagne, the meal timed to the second by the microwave's ping. He doesn't trust the timer and keeps one eye on his watch for fear of dire consequences. It's a microwave, not the Large Hadron Collider, I tell him. We are cooking up paella not black holes. He'll never change.

All of which shenanigans endorses my view that excessive adherence to punctuality carries its own peculiar drawbacks. But I am in my father's son and it is perhaps inevitable that many of his anxieties have transferred to me. When I receive an invitation saying 'seven thirty for eight', I agonise over the precise time at which to arrive. Seven thirty is clearly out of the question. Usually the hosts are running so late that they are probably not yet in their glad rags. They won't thank you if they are forced to answer the door in their underwear. And in any case arriving at seven thirty just makes you look terminally needy. Eight o'clock is for showoffs, those needing to make a grand entrance when all other guests have arrived. Equally needy. Seven forty five then? Well no actually -- that looks too calculating, and smacks of clock watching. In fact all times that are multiples of five minutes are out for the same reason.

So my years of painstaking research have led me to the conclusion that the correct time to arrive at a party is precisely seven forty nine. This conveys to your hosts that you do not wish to encumber them by arriving early, nor do you need to have everyone's attention by arriving late, nor do you clock watch at all. It just looks cool and casual. Of course this kind of relaxed approach requires split-second timing and therefore intense attention to the clock. You might want to consider doing a dry run just to make sure the timings work. I'm sure my father would do. Except of course, he would have arrived at seven twenty nine and fifty nine seconds.

So we Parkies watch the clock. We take tablets by the clock. We note each symptom by the clock. Everything is precise, neither late or early. All by the clock. We wait for a cure. Maybe today? Perhaps tomorrow? Next week then?

How long then?

Tick-tock.

November

I have noticed a difference in the weather and a difference in me. On the whole, it's been a warm October but a sudden nip in the air tells me that autumn is upon us. As sure as the leaves falling from the trees and the recurrence of my great aunt Kath's lumbago, my symptoms change with the seasons. Like a dog wagging its tail, somehow shivers dovetail with tremors and my morning stiffness is exacerbated by the chill. Like the neighbour's car coughing into life each morning, I take an age to waken and move. The summer wardrobe of T shirts and shorts is abandoned and the jumpers emerge from aestivation. I need a winter coat and decide, on a whim to buy a World War Two bomber jacket. Made of thick leather lined with sheepskin, it weighs 15 lbs and is gloriously warm. Not just in temperature, more the kind of comforting warmth of a steaming bath or a mother's hugs. Bingo – all tremors gone!

MISTAKE
Tuesday, 2 November 2010

There are some mistakes you only ever make once. The consequences of your mistake are so extreme, so uniquely memorable that you never ever do the same thing again. Mine was on 15th February 1972.

I forgot my mother's birthday.

That's right. The day after Valentine's Day so you would think that might serve as an effective cue, no? So, no excuses then. I was away at boarding school but still had access to a post office.

Actually I did send my mother a card. I posted it at midday the previous day. And this was in the days when the Royal Mail more or less guaranteed overnight delivery. Especially for bills. So I never gave it a second thought. Card posted. Job done.

But somewhere on a remote Pacific island, a butterfly flapped its wings and unleashed consequences of unimaginable import. The Royal Mail picked this day of all days to not deliver my mother's birthday card.

I know all about disclaimers – that "Ninety five percent of letters are delivered next day, sir".

"Never mind that" I said "You haven't got to face my mother...."

The fact that I can remember the precise date of my misdemeanour so clearly after nearly forty years gives you some indication of the consequences of my action, the magnitude of the transgression.

When the first post arrived and a sheaf of cards tumbled onto the mat, mine did not. Nor did it arrive along with the bills and letters in the second post towards midday. If ever there was a day one wished for third post, this was it. When, at lunchtime, I phoned my mother to wish her a happy birthday, I nonchalantly enquired if she had received my card. To say her response was frosty is akin to saying the Pliocene glaciation was a bit of a cold snap. Her ability to imbue a simple two letter word with such meaning remains a feat to rival Gielgud's Hamlet for expressivity.

No ranting and raving, just clipped monosyllabic answers to my enquiries about her health, what gifts she had received and her choice of dining venue that evening. I explained that I had posted the card the previous day but none of this mattered one jot. There was no card from her firstborn. I was in the doghouse. Not only was I made aware that I had fallen some way short of filial expectations, but there was no indication when the Iron Curtain might be lifted.

In fact the non-arrival of my card was merely the third event in a hat-trick of mishaps that day. Unknown to me, she had scraped her car in the supermarket car park that morning. On returning home, she also discovered that the freezer had packed up. A week earlier. The smell that greeted her on opening it made her vegetarian for a month. So the failure of the Royal Mail to deliver my card was merely the icing on cake so to speak.

The following day my carefully chosen card did arrive and, thanks be to God, had a discernible postmark that verified my story. I was forgiven. My mother was all sweetness and light. She even made a joke of it. Unlike her birthday when I wouldn't have fancied my chances of living through the day.

Many years later I made light of it with my mother and asked if she remembered the occasion. Oh yes, she said, very clearly in a voice laden with meaning. End of conversation. We moved on.

With Parkinson's, forgetfulness is part of the territory. Not frank dementia you understand, but certainly an embarrassing capacity to lose track of key dates. Of course this is a male characteristic anyway.

So last Tuesday I found myself standing sheepishly in the florists, looking to retrieve a situation of my own making through an act of apparently spontaneous generosity. I wasn't alone. Also stood at the counter, with an improbably large bouquet of flowers, was a disconsolate young man who I shall call 'Mike', sporting what appeared to be a bruise on his cheek. He managed a wan smile and we shared one of those entirely male conversations. Fourteen words and long pauses that somehow summarised both of our predicaments.

Jon: (nods at flowers) Wife?
Mike: (doesn't look up) Birthday
Jon: Which?
Mike: 30
Jon: (shakes head) Bad
Mike: (nods) Bad. You?
Jon: Anniversary
Mike: Big?
Jon: 20
Mike: (winces) Ooh
Jon: Yes.
Mike: Good luck

FIREWORKS
Sunday, 7 November 2010

You're never too old for fireworks.

It's six thirty on November 5th and, as we have done every year for the last fifteen, the Stamfords are wrapping up in coats, hats and scarves. The annual town fireworks display is due to start in less than an hour and, as old hands at this, we know where to get the best view. If we leave now we will still be able to pitch ourselves down by the lake, close to the action.

Catherine is not with us this evening -- she's up in London, at college, with friends, and hoping to attend two separate fireworks parties. Alice and Alex might just as well not be with us. Alice has a friend, Bella, with her and the two, whispering in quiet agreement, clearly do not intend to spend time with old fogeys like Claire and myself. While Claire and I are donning woolly hats, thick gloves and wellies, Alice and Bella are discussing the comparative merits of Urban Decay or Fuschia Falls mascara. Clearly there will be boys at the fireworks and the need to look beautiful outweighs the more mundane considerations of keeping chills at bay. Gloves are out of the question – nails must be visible and the choice between Cocoa Bliss, Confident Coral or Winter Berries nail varnish must be addressed. I inquire whether the cosmetic range includes Frostbite Blue or Chilblain Cherry and am given the kind of look that would turn milk sour. Teenage daughters are a different species.

Footwear discussions fare little better. It has rained for three days and the park, churned up by a legion of feet will be a quagmire. Strappy sandals are as appropriate here as Doc Martins at a Berkeley Square ball. I put my foot down so to speak and insist on trainers at the very least. Alice accedes under protest, muttering to Bella. A stick of chewing gum apiece, and their ensembles are complete.

Alex and his friend Tom are in many ways just as difficult. Alex seems to be affecting a kind of Polish immigrant fruitpicker chic at the moment, consisting of a mixture of Arctic camouflage and Dayglo Lycra. Nothing matches. That would be too obvious. Tom looks like an off-duty Formula One driver but has no hat. I offer him a Jaguar woolly and the look of disdain is fleeting but obvious. In many ways the sartorial antithesis of Bronislaw, or whoever Alex is this week, Tom would not be seen dead in a garment branded by the wrong automotive product. And for an officianado of the Bayerischer Motor Werke's design studio, Jaguar is emphatically the wrong label. Besides it's British. I treat Tom to a history lesson, reminding him that Jaguars are built in the same factory that once made Spitfires, but he is unmoved. He wears the hat inside out to disguise the label.

Eventually we leave the house, me whistling a medley of tunes from The Battle of Britain, 633 Squadron and The Dambusters. A throng are slowly making their way up the hill to the park. We have barely gone twenty yards when Alice and Bella run into friends and separate from our party. It seems orchestrated, with hindsight. So suddenly we are not six but four. At the top of the road, Bronislaw asks for the £5 entrance fee 'in case we get separated'. Twenty yards further and Bronislaw and Jenson Button are nowhere to be seen and it is just Claire and me.

The park is full to bursting with the usual sideshows -- candy floss, flashing Viking helmets and fairy wings, luminescent balloons, sparklers, and the kind of hot dogs and burgers that rightly give Britain its reputation as a culinary desert. We weave our way among the young and old, briefly spotting Alice and, to her horror, calling her name and waving at her. "Who's the old shaky?" you can almost sense her friends asking her.

Our usual spot, toward the lake and not far from an ageing beech tree, is occupied by a giggling group of gum-chewing young girls, with camera phones, each surreptitiously checking their makeup. To their left stand the cream of the town's male youth, teenage boys clumsily affecting the kind of nonchalant mien perfected by James Dean. Except that none of them would have a clue who James Dean was. Besides, James Dean never dressed at Top Man. They are passing round a can of supermarket lager one has sneaked through security. Each tribe feigns indifference to the other.

Wafted from further still, among the smoke from the burger van, there is a distinct whiff of something like burning leaves.

"What's that smell? " asks Claire.

"Herbal cigarettes" I venture, recognising instantly the smell of cannabis. We move along, in a vain attempt to find a viewing place free from the maelstrom of hormones and hemp that seems to be the hallmark of this evening.

The PA system is raucous, booming and the DJ largely unintelligible. The hip-hop eventually stops and the music from 2001 A Space Odyssey signals the imminent beginning of the fireworks. Twenty minutes of feedback and distortion later, it's all over. Our ears are ringing to the sound of Star Wars and our retinas are scored with the potassium pinks, copper blues and sodium yellows of the fireworks. Claire and I look at each other. Not as many loud bangs as usual we agree, not that you would have heard them over the ear bleeding drivel from the PA. But even visually there was less variety, less interest, and less drama. "More daisies than chrysanthemums," as Claire put it. Maybe this is a recession firework display?

Back at the house, our errant offspring magically reappear. Alex and Tom are waiting outside the house, lured by the promise of takeaway pizza. Alice and Bella return later, the wanton calories of pizza less of a draw. Tom is just glad to be rid of the Jaguar hat. Fireworks over for another year.

Of course the best firework display I ever saw was on 4 July 1988, in Indiana. Always spectacular, the Independence Day celebration that year excelled itself not only for the magnificence of the display but also for its brevity. Using a complex but novel electronic ignition system, the event was planned to choreograph an ever-changing array of colours and shapes in the night sky. The organisers even had an animation video, shown at the local shopping mall to whet the appetite. It looked stunning and I could hardly wait for the real thing.

The real thing itself was infinitely more spectacular than the video, and a world removed from anything the organisers could have imagined. Two enormous Mack trucks and their trailers formed a giant launch platform for the evening's pyrotechnics. Unknown to the organisers, a raccoon had gnawed through the cable, shorting the ignition sequencer and detonating all $54,000 worth of fireworks at the same time. The resulting display -- if display is the word -- lasted 11 seconds but lit up the night sky in a way that had the National Guard briefly mobilised. For the Army and Navy veterans, camped in wheelchairs in the front rows, it was all too much. Suddenly they were back at Pearl Harbor. When the smoke cleared, all you could see were the burning trailers of the trucks.

You're never too old for fireworks.

MOTHER
Unpublished, November 2010

The cemetery is mostly modern, municipal and managed. In the older part, yew trees grow in cultured isolation whilst, even in the newer areas, bushes and shrubs soften the open landscape. It may not be Highgate, San Michele or Pere Lachaise but it means more to me than all of these.

It's been a little over a year since we buried my mother. A year in which her corner of the cemetery has gradually filled up, barely a week unmarked by the cutting of the sod. Alone last November, she is spoilt for company now as death takes its inexorable toll.

The grave is no longer a brutal earthy scar in the grass. There is a gravestone now, a plain limestone slab with a simple statement of her dates and a quotation. Nothing ostentatious – we are of Northern stock and do not hold with fancy monuments or saccharine sentiments. The words "There is no death, only a change of worlds" were chosen by my brother from a native American text and perfectly express the cycle of life and death.

I visit the grave every so often. Sometimes I leave flowers – on her birthday and so forth – but mostly I just stop by for a few words. I kneel quietly and tell her our news, what the children are doing and so on. And I try to tell her how much I miss her.

But she knows that.

December

The snow came early this year, fleeting flurries at first, giving way to large plopping flakes and clumps as the ground whitened and softened. It snowed all night and, by morning, the landscape was like an iced cake. The weather forecast said more was coming. It was right.

By nightfall, the street was silent, no marks in the virgin snow. I thought of past Christmases, of childhood Yuletides, of woolly caps and gloves, runny noses, chilblains and snowball fights. Children slip, slide and stagger, teeter and topple, their reeling gait and unsteady steps lending them a foolishness I thought mine and mine alone.

Welcome to my world.

BOTCHED
Wednesday, 1 December 2010

There is a certain kind of person who should just never attempt DIY. They should never pick up a screwdriver, Allen key, or hammer. Especially the hammer, that weapon of last resort too often mistaken as the tool of first resort. I am one of those people and, for the most part, I manage successfully to abrogate my DIY responsibilities with a series of other diversionary activities. It's for the best really, because with my basement level of mechanical aptitude, injury and damage is almost guaranteed. I am pathologically incapable of putting together even the most trivial cabinet without the resultant edifice collapsing or requiring additional structural support. I often wonder where the house and contents policy ends.

The sight of me in Homebase or B&Q is as pitiful as it gets. Shop assistants circle around me like hammerheads round a stricken tuna, seemingly determined to confuse me with helpful advice. Even the language of DIY bewilders me -- it's all widgets, sprockets and dowels. Then there are the spigots, gimlets and grommets. How are you meant to remember this stuff? I couldn't tell an auger bit from a bolster chisel, an eye bolt from a gland valve, or a shavehook from a bradawl. Hell, I don't even know my noggings from my purlins. How feeble is that.

It was no better when I was younger. My carpentry teacher Mr Murray still remembers me to this day, forty years later, so deeply is my woodwork imprinted on his psyche. One has the sense that some sins are never forgiven. Whilst the rest of the class were producing beautiful dovetail joints, hinges and finials to his cooing satisfaction, I was cobbling together a small bookcase that lent a new definition to the word rustic. When I eventually submitted it for the teacher's scrutiny, there were so many protruding nails that he immediately christened it The Porcupine. Forget your Arts and Crafts, Chippendale or Sheraton, my approach to furniture building, a technique based entirely around the use of needlessly lengthy nails, could have founded a new school of design. Always assuming of course that anybody actually wanted furniture that drew blood.

And of course with Parkinson's, there is a certain imprecision about movements, lending a further air of tension to the simple act of tapping in a nail. The likelihood of the hammer head striking the right sort of nail is at best a fifty-fifty throw. So many attempts to wield a hammer end with crushed fingers and thumbs.

Of course much of this could be avoided, or so I'm reliably assured, if one was female. Females apparently read the instructions whereas, as any man will tell you, the instructions are for wimps, to be consulted only after the screwdriver has failed to cut the mustard. Although, even then, there is always the hammer.

Still, all this was ancient history -- or so I thought when Alice asked me if I could assemble her new furniture. IKEA flatpack apparently, and 'ridiculously easy' to assemble, according to Alice. Claire told me that 'even a trained monkey could put it together', a pronouncement somehow not quite affording me the level of confidence that I had anticipated. I suggested that, in that event, they should investigate the range of simian carpentry services available in the Yellow Pages. Alice's response, along the lines of 'just get on with it and don't be a smartass' led me to conclude that further procrastination would be unproductive.

The moment I laid out the instructions on the floor of Alice's bedroom, I found myself having a flashback. I was in the bathroom of our last house, dripping with sweat, and stepping back to admire the bathroom cabinet I had not only assembled successfully but also attached firmly to the bathroom wall. Upside down.

The flashbacks came thick and fast -- Catherine's slatted bed, where my failure to anchor the slats to the frame had woken us in the middle of the night to the sound of Catherine falling through the bed, like a scene from The Omen. Or perhaps my first encounter with the awesome destructive potential of the jigsaw, my attempts to trim a complex shape in hardboard inevitably costing us six inches of the patio table. Or even my attempt to regrout that single tile in the bathroom, a five-minute job at best, but in my hands an effort which somehow managed to detach a further eleven tiles into a heap of broken porcelain on the floor. My wife, hearing the noise asked if everything was okay. 'Just be a few minutes more dear' I replied with what I hoped sounded a cheerily reassuring tone. It evidently wasn't and I heard Claire coming upstairs to check. Fortunately I made it to the lock first and encouraged her not to enter for her own safety because there were 'tools all over the floor'. Not to mention broken tiles. It is a measure of my discomfiture that for several seconds I contemplated leaving the bathroom by the window. Along with getting in a car and driving until the petrol ran out.

As I sat looking at the parts for Alice's bookcase, the tension was palpable. But this would be different, a team effort. Alice and I would cover for each other and, by exhaustive and painstaking quality-control, we would ensure that the final result was a bookcase to be proud of. In one fell swoop, I would exorcise all my DIY ghosts.

An hour later, and without even resorting to the hammer except where instructed, the bookcase was finished. We pulled it up right and it stood like the monolith in 2001, a testament to the indomitable will and design skills of IKEA. Sadly also a testament to the breathtaking incompetence of a father and daughter. The moment the bookcase was vertical, it was apparent that two of the shelves had been put in back to front. Instead of a pale beech veneer, we were facing unadorned fibreboard. It was The Porcupine all over again. Moreover, because of the tap-in shelf locks, there was no way to retrieve the situation. Alice and I looked at each other as we heard Claire coming upstairs.

But whilst I may not be able to put furniture together correctly, I have become, through necessity, a master at blagging my way out of DIY trouble. Alice and I headed to B&Q on the flimsy pretext of needing a 'ZP 443 ratchet screwdriver'. Twenty minutes later we had smuggled the sticky back plastic into her bedroom and, as fortune would have it, it was an excellent match. Another five minutes and we had covered our tracks, the back to front shelves looked indistinguishable from the rest of the bookcase. Even Claire was impressed. 'Not your usual botched job' she said, keen not to overegg the pudding with fulsome praise.

As she left the room to cook lunch, Alice and I breathed a collective sigh of relief. And for me it was even better -- I had found somebody who was even more incompetent at DIY than myself. If she weren't my daughter I would still love her.

THE CHICK MAGNET
Thursday, 9 December 2010

Alex was looking perplexed in the bathroom mirror. "It's just a spot" I said. Alex rolled his eyes upwards "Oh God, puberty -- that's all I need!" Especially after the surprise physics test the previous day. Could life be any worse?

Children grow up only to quickly these days. Before you know it they have stopped playing with train sets and are asking you those embarrassing questions along the lines of "where did I come from?" I was about halfway through explaining this in what I thought was honest if rather biological language when Alex stopped me. "It's just that Sanjay comes from Karachi," he said "and I wondered where I was from." I breathed a sigh of relief. "Oh, and dad, enough of the sex education please -- there are children present!"

I abandon the sex education, thankful that I didn't need recourse to pamphlets, or worse still, the lyrics to early Motown albums. I still treated him to a metaphorical clip around the ear for being a smartass.

Still, there comes a point when you realise that your little boy is not a little boy any more. There are tell-tale signs not only that they are growing up but that this process has crept up on you much faster than the anticipated. Much like the nesting behaviour exhibited by pregnant women shortly before birth, there are clear behavioural patterns exhibited by the adolescent boy. Apart from the obvious vocal changes -- our neighbour's boy went from Jimmy Somerville to Barry White overnight -- there are so many mental and emotional adjustments to be made. Some of these directly impinge upon me. Most notably, my aftershave is going down much faster than usual. I seriously wonder whether he's drinking the stuff.

The road to adulthood for boys is fraught with pitfalls and perils. There are choices to make, paths to walk and much to learn. School is there to help turn the boy into the man, to guide and advise along that path. But ultimately, a son turns to his father for guidance and any father worth his salt should be ready with the answers. I need to be there for Alex in the same way that Homer is for Bart.

Okay that's probably not the best example.

And of course as his father I have some words of advice.

Firstly, the mere fact that girls of the same age are prepared to talk to you does not make you 'a chick magnet' (your words not mine). Only people in Carry On films talk like that. Stop it now.

Secondly, despite the advertising, spraying Lynx into the air in sufficient quantities to rupture the ozone layer will not have attractive young women battering down the bathroom door like Parkie babes on dopamine agonists. We call that advertising -- it's not real. Unlike the hole in the ozone layer now over Kent.

Thirdly, on that same note, treat girlfriends a darn sight better than you treat your sisters. Then treat your sisters better. Believe me, you're going to need them.

Fourthly, stop using my aftershave -- buy your own. Or wait until you are shaving. And don't even think of using my razorblades.

Fifthly, if you fret over a single pimple today, you will not believe the facial Armageddon that is in store. Remember the scene in Poltergeist? It's worse.

Finally, make sure you clear the search history on Google. You're not the only one who uses the computer.

I'm not finished with the parental wisdom but that'll do for now.

I'll be back.

THE POST OFFICE
Wednesday, 15 December 2010

I have to be honest -- I really don't like post offices. No matter how trivial or simple my requirements, the Post Office seems to have a way of conspiring to crush them. In bygone days where there were separate queues for each position, I would invariably be standing behind the person who wanted to change nationality. Or a man determined to pay in the contents of nineteen fruit machines. Or even, and I recollect it with a wry smile, there would be that blank faced little man with Parkinson's, fumbling for an eternity to find a few coins necessary to buy a stamp. If nothing else Parkinson's has taught me the value of patience. Undignified though it is, at least the cattle grid system ensures that for the most part you won't be stuck behind Parkie Jon. Except of course at the local post office near us, where there is a distinct possibility. Especially on Thursday.

So last Thursday, as everyone queues to send Christmas cards to bizarre foreign locations, I stand shivering and shaking between a Giles cartoon granny with a bag of mint imperials and a couple of cheery but grimy new-age travellers. There is no heating in the Post Office and we can see our breath on this icy December morning. Two ahead of me is a dishevelled young girl, perhaps no more than eighteen, with two small children writhing in a buggy. Even my blunted sense of smell alerts me to the fact that their nappies need changing. She is clearly in need of nicotine and impatiently rolls a cigarette between her fingers as the toddlers squabble.

We are all cold and in a hurry.

Holding court at the front of the queue is a well-known local drug addict, who has been waiting for twenty minutes to cash his giro which is "f***ing out of order". As the methadone wears off, he becomes increasingly agitated and abusive. The Giles granny switches off her hearing aid. Just as he launches another cold turkey tirade, spitting at the nervous till assistant, the police arrive. Six police officers, batons and pepper spray at the ready. They are visibly disappointed. This is the second time in a week and they are fed up of Frankie.

The collective sigh of relief from the queue is short lived as the police usher everyone outside while they "deal with the situation". It has started to snow again and whilst it was cold inside, outside is worse. The granny, who has no gloves, had only nipped out to buy the mints and is not dressed for a blizzard. I tap on the door and politely suggest that the police interview the drug addict outside, while we buy our Christmas stamps. The drug addict is having none of this and proceeds to treat the constables to another stream of profanities, mostly focused on their sexual proclivities and dubious parentage.

The police officers, irrespective of their parentage, explain to him that, in their considered opinion, silence is golden. I'm paraphrasing here -- the officers don't mince their words. Frankie still doesn't take their cue. Suddenly, he is pinned to the floor like an Atlas butterfly and manacled. Even for a man apparently so well versed in the law of the land, he is quick to inform us that this infringes his human rights. Most of the queue, his captive audience, freezing quietly in the snow, feel that Frankie is long overdue for a bit of infringing.

And, he is at pains to assure us, he'll be writing to his MP about the shoddy service received from the Post Office. The till girl says that he can write all he pleases but he won't get a stamp to post it. But Frankie has moved on and is now ranting on about the summary justice meted out to him by the Constabulary. Just as he starts a prolonged vernacular outburst about wasting taxpayers' money, the Giles granny reminds him that he doesn't pay tax and therefore might be best advised to keep his counsel. She waves Frankie goodbye as he is bundled into the back of a Panda.

"That took you long time" says Claire, as I shake the snow off my boots in the porch.

"Sorry about that" I reply "bit of a queue".

TWO JAGS
Monday, 20 December 2010

As readers of *Slice of Life* may remember, one of my earliest responses to being diagnosed with Parkinson's was to buy myself a Jag. Not, in fairness, an impulse purchase although you could be forgiven for thinking that, considering the volume of dopamine agonists I take. No, I had always promised myself a Jag when I retired but, as so often with Parkinson's, events overtake us. In all likelihood, by the time I reach retirement age in a decade or so time, I will no longer be driving. So, in 2007, it was a case of "Carpe Diem" and a zircon blue three litre S-Type.

I have driven many cars over the years. That said, the Jag has been unequivocally the most mechanically tetchy car I have ever owned, seeming to spend half its time at the garage for one niggle after another. Exasperating, high maintenance and ludicrously thirsty. A ridiculous indulgence by any rational standard. Yet, at the same time, it has been the car that put a smile on my face like no other. A thrill to drive. A car that, with its feline suppleness, somehow seemed to make up for my Parkinson's stiffness. Even Claire and the kids grudgingly accepted the cat as a member of our extended family menagerie. And for Alex, it ramped up his playground credibility a notch or two.

I had always thought that the car would see me to the end of my motoring days. Some sort of compensation for a lifetime of horrid hatchbacks, scrappy saloons, and crummy coupes. I knew my motoring days would not be forever. I had even mentally prepared for the day when I would finally hand back my driving licence and let go of the car. A rite of passage certainly, unwelcome but not unexpected.

Completely unexpected, by comparison, is the blue Toyota emerging at speed from a side road, straight into the side of the Jag on the Wednesday morning school run. In the blink of an eye, that is that. Fortunately the kids are not in the car. The other driver makes off. Phone calls to the insurance company then off to the police station to make a statement.

In the new spirit of engagement, we are invited to be involved more investigations, it seems. "What action would you like to see with regards to the third-party?" The officer asks me. Not being in much of a turn-the-other-cheek mood, "I'd like to see his testicles taken off with a band saw, fried in butter and fed back to him" I think to myself. Fortunately this comes out as "that's for you to decide after weighing the evidence, officer". We fill out a seemingly endless incident report form, tick hundreds of boxes and sign endless pages.

Finally, understandably misinterpreting my shakes, he hands me a leaflet about victim support and briefly details my eligibility for counselling. The Jag is loaded onto the back of a trailer, and off to the garage. An hour later, a perfunctory phone call from the garage and the car is a write-off. I hadn't even got my CDs out of the glove compartment.

Despite their well intended if misplaced generosity, I decide not to take the police up on their offer of counselling. No, the solution is made clear to me by Alice, my equestrian daughter. Like a rider bucked by a horse, I decide the best policy is to get back in the saddle.

This poses a financial conundrum. Once you have owned a Jag, there is no way back. I phone Claire to tell her that I'm thinking about another Jag. Her response is, at best, lukewarm. Only after I put the phone down, does it occur to me that I should have mentioned the crash first. I phone again and explain that I am not having a John Prescott moment -- this is a replacement not an addition, since the S type is, as of today, scrap. "How convenient" she replies, still unconvinced. I make a mental note to buy flowers.

I phone the Jag garage. No S-Types in my price range. Would I be interested in upgrading, they enquire. Before I can say no, the salesman has reeled off the key features of a newly arrived 2006 XJ. There is no escaping the fact that it's very attractively priced but still, tantalisingly, just out of my price range. But that does not stop me requesting a test drive. The salesman is surprisingly accommodating. In fact, so keen is the chap that he offers to bring it round to my house that evening.

It's hard to escape a feeling of déjà vu when the car arrives outside. It's even the same colour as the S-Type, albeit much larger. It drives like a flying carpet, smooth and refined but with enough grunt to surprise. Like the S-Type before it, I know instantly that I want it. But how do I break it to the salesman that I simply cannot afford the car? He's unlikely to be amused at the thought of his evening wasted without hope of a sale.

Fate intervenes.

With a week left in the month, it turns out the salesman is one short on his quota for November. His annual bonus more or less hangs on the car and he is as keen to sell as I am to buy. Unashamedly, I take full advantage. A grand off the asking price? No problem. Taxed? Certainly. A year's warranty? Of course. MOT? Naturally. A full valet? Without question. He will even pay for a couple of weeks' insurance to get it off the forecourt.

We shake. Hands in his case, entire body in mine -- I'm that excited.

BAH HUMBUG!
Friday, 24 December 2010

It's the same every Christmas. There is one thing that I dread more than any other about the festive season. One thing that can single-handedly nullify all the carefully nurtured good cheer and bonhomie. One small miserable fly in the ointment of universal goodwill. Care to guess?

No, although I fully sympathise with you, the answer is not sprouts.

I'm talking about something far worse even than sprouts, if such a thing is imaginable. The nameless horror of which I speak is pantomime. Actually that should not be pantomime so much as Pantomime. The former merely signifies, in the generic sense, communication by means of gesture and facial expression, a noble tradition rooted in Greco-Roman history. But the latter Pantomime (with a capital P), in my humble opinion, goes far beyond that and affords one of the most unsettling insights currently available into the British collective psyche. Psychologists and psychiatrists would have, indeed do have, a field day.

What might they make of a drama in which the leading male role must be played by a comely girl and where the heroine's stepsisters are played by front row forwards from the local rugby club in drag, to say nothing of the roll call of "celebrities" earning most of their annual crust over the Christmas period. I can't speak for all but I know that this psychologist struggles to see the point. And the incessant tennis of "oh yes it is/oh no it isn't" makes me want to scream "get on with it". Actually it just makes me want to scream. Full stop. And as for pantomime animals, don't get me started. I would need to be sedated to go to all panto, but it would take a chemical cosh to get me through Aladdin.

I should make it clear at this point that, even in my own family, among what you might imagine to be folk of a similar kidney, I am in a minority of one. Claire, Catherine, Alice and Alex all blissfully enjoy the town's annual panto, be it Snow White, Cinderella, or Sleeping

Beauty. Every year they are in the front rows shouting "he's behind you" at 120 dB. But no amount of coaxing by my family will persuade me to join them. Normally happy to attend any credible theatrical diversion, I draw the line at panto. While they troop off in the snow to catch the Boxing Day Sleeping Beauty matinee, I park myself on the sofa with a glass of Talisker and a video documentary of Herbert von Karajan, party animal that I am. Having attended the panto thrice over the last decade, albeit under duress on each occasion, I'm satisfied that I have discharged my Pantomime duties for this lifetime. Having visited Bayreuth several times, Claire feels much the same about Wagner.

It's hard to believe that Pantomime and opera actually derive from a common source, in the same way that birds and dinosaurs share common ancestors. Pantomime in Restoration England began as a series of brief comic dramas breaking up an evening of opera, before eventually becoming separate shows in their own right. These gradually became more topical, theatrical and elaborate, taking on their own distinct and separate identity, costumes and conventions. And audience. By the early 1800s pantomime was more or less a distinctive theatrical form, mercifully reserved for the Christmas period.

Why do I need to be such a curmudgeon, I hear you ask. Why do I feel the need to boo all the characters, not just the baddies? Even Claire, fully cognisant of my own aversion, is bewildered by its extent. Why do I need to be so difficult? It's hard to say but for sheer enjoyment, I would be hard pressed to choose between Pantomime and waterboarding.

Never was this antipathy to panto more sorely tested than in 2003, when Alice and Alex both appeared in the town's production of Snow White, hobnobbing with Anita Dobson and other glitterati of the panto circuit. Up to that point, their dramatic aspirations had been confined to their primary school nativity play. Alice, offered her pick of the roles available, spurned the Virgin Mary (for most young girls a given) and chose a donkey. Specifically the rear half of the donkey. Let's face it, with this kind of casting, even self-imposed, Marlon Brando would have struggled to catch the critic's eye. In any case, so numerous were the pupils at the school and so imperative the need to include all, that the nativity was performed with 15 wise men, 40 angels and a good 20 shepherds all in costumes reminiscent of Yasser Arafat. You couldn't find a tea towel in Tunbridge Wells for love nor money that week. The entire school, some hundred and fifty pupils, were involved in the nativity play in some form, many as animals, or parts of animals. I have seen Aida staged at the Royal Opera House with fewer performers.

Still, when you have been the hindquarters in the donkey, anything is a step up. Alice's 'Third Villager' and Alex's 'Street Urchin #4' were, by general acknowledgement, the thespian highlights of this star-studded soirée, and the crowning glory of their stage aspirations. To this day I am at a loss to know why Alice and Alex were overlooked for the Harry Potter films.

A certain double standard I hear you say. Certainly it's difficult to square my discomfort over pantomime in general with pleasure at watching my children perform on stage. King Lear or Hamlet would have been great but I'm sure that even Lawrence Olivier must have started somewhere

Hamlet: "To be or not to be. That is the question"
Audience: "Oh no it isn't"

MAMMON ON BOXING DAY
Wednesday, 29 December 2010

Christmas Day in the Stamford household is straightforward, prescriptive and routine. Like a well oiled machine, everything occurs on a rigid timetable that changes little from year to year.
1) Wake up
2) Put the turkey in the oven (even though it's still dark outside)
3) Pour yourself a glass of Bucks fizz.
4) Wait for children who despite the best intentions have not woken at the crack of dawn
5) Open the presents, noting who gave what
6) Christmas dinner, swiftly followed by the Queen's speech, chocolates, several glasses of port and the first couple of hours of the Melbourne test match.

Boxing Day, by comparison, is a very different beast. Or at least it is in our house if we do not have guests. Firstly there is no structure at all to the day. There are no meals today. Instead the family scavenges like buzzards. Turkey sandwiches, reheated Christmas pudding, satsumas and liqueur chocolates provide an incongruous, if strangely balanced, diet.

Claire and I wake as usual with the light. As so often, apart from the hens and the occasional more inquisitive guinea pig, nothing else stirs. By eight, I have already completed the only urgent business of the day, returning from the garage with milk, bread and most of the world reserves of AA batteries.

Catherine, Alice and Alex are all still asleep three hours later. Alice is the first to stir, bemoaning the unwanted, if imperceptible, weight gain from yesterday. She leaves Claire and I in no doubt over the extent of our culpability. Even so, and faced with the cornucopia of calories available in the house, she is weighing up the comparative merits of grapefruit segments or Thornton's fudge for breakfast. It does not take a genius to predict the outcome. Equally predictable are the hours of vocal self loathing that ensue. I retire to the shed with a weapons grade espresso.

Alex surfaces bleary eyed towards midday, switches on the computer, television, toaster, radio and Xbox before pouring himself some milk. He leaves the fridge door open, lights the gas hob and water for pasta. It is clear, even at thirteen, that he will have no difficulty adapting to life as a student. As the water boils, he watches the cricket highlights from Australia. Claire, sipping her tea, asks if he has done any music practice this holiday (his trumpet teacher is frustrated by his lack of progress. And attendance). His response, the first sounds uttered by him thus far, and delivered entirely in grunts, confirms that he has not. At which point he is cordially invited to rectify the situation and we are treated to loud, petulant and perfunctory renditions of 'O Sole Mio' and 'Tuxedo Junction'. As Claire and I are nursing hangovers (whose idea was the absinthe anyway?), the wisdom of our request is at best questionable. Just as he begins another nerve jangling trumpet involuntary, we decide enough is enough and beg him to stop.

Catherine joins us in the early afternoon, just as I, hangover improved, stand poised with the Wagner CD to smoke her out. She is of course already a student and therefore has no circadian rhythm. To her, 2 PM is early and she is at a loss to explain the presence of her entire family, already dressed. Still in her pyjamas, she flops onto the sofa with a laptop and an iTunes voucher. A few mouse clicks, and she is the proud owner of what I am assured is the 'critically acclaimed' debut album by Black Parrot Seaside and the Exploding Sheep (or something similar). I can hardly contain my indifference. She closes the laptop like an aluminium clam and joins Alice at the dining room table, nonchalantly thumbing the latest Tommy Hilfiger and Jack Wills catalogues. Several thousand pounds worth of window shopping later, and the girls have mapped out the remainder of their day to their satisfaction. Their original plan, to go skiing at a nearby dry ski slope, has been thwarted by heavy snow at the ski centre which has closed the piste. The girls opt for retail therapy.

The January sales, for reasons incomprehensible to me, start on Boxing Day. I rashly offer to drive the girls to the shopping precinct which, bearing in mind the gridlock on the roads, turns out to be a feat akin to walking on water. There is nowhere to park and the town is full of grinning people wearing improbably patterned jumpers, socks or comical ties. It is like a cross between Blue Peter and a Hieronymus Bosch painting and, at the same time, a sneak preview of the Oxfam Winter collection. Those fortunate enough still to have the receipts for their woollens are queueing at the returns desk. My friend Zak's grandmother, with undiagnosed Alzheimer's at the time, took such decisive exception to the pale peach cardigan bought for her one Christmas that she returned it to the shop for a refund, after lecturing Zak at length over his insensitive colour choice. A week later, oblivious or unrepentant, she returned to the shop with her thirty five p£35 and bought the same cardy at half price in the sale, splashing the balance on scratchcards and a bottle of supermarket gin.

Unable to find a parking space, despite circling the town like a jumbo jet waiting to land at Heathrow, I abandon the girls in town to flex their plastic. By sleeping through the early part of the day, Catherine and Alice have missed the inevitable ugly scenes at the department stores where buyers brawl over bargains in an unseemly orgy of consumerism. Probably just as well -- you wouldn't want to be the one standing between Alice and a half price Gucci handbag.

It's no better at the industrial estate where televisions, fridges, microwaves and laptops are leaving the shops faster than at Toxteth in 1981, an endless procession of 4x4s filled with a flurry of white goods. I briefly nip into Halfords to collect new headlamp bulbs, the entire process taking twenty minutes -- one minute to select the bulbs and nineteen queueing to pay. I resolve, as I do every year, never to shop in the sales. Shops seething with people barging their way from bargain to bargain are bad enough for the able-bodied but, to those of us of a shaky persuasion, can so easily end with a fall, especially when you add ice from slippery boots to the equation.

Paralysed by sleepiness, the result of a sedative symbiosis of dopamine agonists and Pinot Grigio, I doze on the sofa, dreaming in black and white of 1930s Doncaster and of railway families scrimping and saving to buy school shoes, in the last great depression. My grandparents in essence. The doorbell rings and I am woken by the girls returning from town, laden with designer bags like Prada pack mules. Alice is ecstatic.

"Dad, you wouldn't believe how much we saved"

"Surprise me" I say.

January

I am tired, dog-tired
With aching marrow and flint-sharpened flats
Swollen puttied ankles and heavy legs
Soft slipper shuffles, trips and tumbles
Fading voice and pill-slurred mumbles
Am I alone to think these thoughts
To jump at shapes, freeze with night's shadows
As day brings night, fatigued and frightened
Already taut tendons tightened
Until the greying puddle of dawn
Greeted with eyes open, back turned
Day's mother cuddles, darkness crumbles

REFLECTIONS AND RESOLUTIONS
Saturday, 1 January 2011

Yes it's that time of year -- a time for maudlin introspection as, glass of something medicinal in hand, we review the past and gaze on the future, all to the sound of Auld Lang Syne.

I suppose it's a convenient point, but the end of one year and the beginning of another always seems to be a moment to take stock and reflect on the world, the family and one's own circumstances. How many of last year's resolutions and aspirations still hold? How many will hold a year from now? How many of our dreams have been fulfilled and stand proud and tall, confident affirmations of our identity? How many lie broken, dashed on the rocks of life, or tucked away, shaming indictments of our inadequacies?

For many, our resolutions are perennial -- to lose weight, to be a better parent/spouse/sibling, and so forth. Some resolutions go beyond the personal battles. For some, this is not a personal battle against Parkinson's but a war on behalf of many. Perhaps you resolved to take the fight to the enemy by raising funds for research or raising awareness of the condition. Perhaps you intended to run marathons. Or maybe jump out of aeroplanes. Or cycle around the coast of Britain. Maybe you had smaller but equally noble aspirations. But life got in the way perhaps. Or time passed and before you knew it, the year had gone.

So don't turn your back on your good intentions. Don't condemn yourself as a failure. Don't be hard on yourself now because you were soft on yourself then. Think of it is postponed rather than cancelled.

So dust those resolutions down, shake off the cobwebs and polish them up. Make 2011 the year of forgotten resolutions. Look back in those diaries at the words you wrote this time last year and the year before. Think of it as a second chance. Sometimes we will be able to help in ways we had not expected. But above all, it behoves us all, as individuals as well as members of the wider Parkinson's community, to help in whatever ways we can.

Join a clinical trial perhaps? Cheer people up with your writing? Raise money for research? Tell your story and make people aware of Parkinson's? Run, skip, jump, anything. No matter what you do, resolve to make a difference

I resolve in 2011 to make a difference. In some small way, I will make a difference to people with Parkinson's. Be it ever so small, and affecting ever so few, I will still make a difference. Whether as a scientist, an artist, a reader or writer, by fundraising or other means, to make a difference on the journey to a cure.

I will not forget. I will tie a knot in my handkerchief. I will make a note in my diary. I will stick a post it note on my computer. Even as the fireworks ring out, and the champagne flows, I will not forget.

It is 2011 and I resolve to make a difference.

HAPPY HOUR
Wednesday, 5 January 2011

The Christmas and New Year period is increasingly a season of excess. I accept that. I concede that I will be five pounds heavier in January than I was in December and that most of that can be attributed to my own breathtaking lack of willpower. If food is put in front of me I will eat it. End of story. Faced with so many delicious things, it's only fair to try all. Quails eggs, caviar, smelly French cheeses, you name it -- the list goes on, and so does my consumption.

But when it comes to Christmas drinks, the contrast could not be more striking. Here you find me strangely conservative. At any party, I am happy with a glass of honest bitter or a decent bottle of claret. Or a snifter of a good single malt will do me quite nicely thank you. But here, as so often in life, it seems I cut a lonely furrow. While I am sat in a corner at the office party with a glass of Talisker, friends and colleagues order a rainbow of bizarrely coloured and suggestively named cocktails. "What are you drinking?" I ask one young lady with a luminous green drink. "A Passionate Shag on the Piano" she replies, with the kind of laugh that shatters windows. I briefly toy with the idea of asking the ingredients but in the end decide that I don't actually care what some tittering clot in marketing had done to come up with this.

Personally I blame all those funny coloured or odd flavoured liqueurs that appear at Christmas. I mean, I ask you, who drinks ginger wine except at Christmas? And blue Curaçao -- what is that about? Crème de menthe? Don't get me started. Somehow the moment it's Christmas, we feel the need to subject our already more fragile selves to drinks we wouldn't touch at any other time of year. And this behaviour is not confined to the work environment. Maiden aunts, normally starchily abstemious, suddenly feel the need to drink Snowballs, Screaming Orgasms or Blue Lagoons. Things with pineapple, glace cherries and parasols. Things best left where they originated. Let's face it - a Mai Tai served by some dusky grass skirted maiden on Waikiki beach may be quite a life enhancing experience. The same cannot be said for the selfsame drink at an office party, cobbled together around cheap gin and tinned pineapple chunks by Beryl from accounts. And we shouldn't be surprised if that wonderful Provencal Pastis, sipped at sunset from a terrace bar overlooking lavender fields in Rocamadour fails to weave quite the same spell on a cold, wet Sunday afternoon in Salford. These things have a time and place and are best left in that time and that place. As happy memories.

So why do we seek out these strange concoctions? Well, it will come as no surprise to you to learn that this is the result of high levels of activity in one particular part of the brain. And more than that, to one single neurotransmitter. The part of the brain in question is the limbic system and the neurotransmitter responsible -- I'm sure you've already guessed -- is that old devil called dopamine.

The wanton desire to try out new experiences, for no reason other than the fact that they are new, is what scientists call novelty seeking behaviour. It is related to other behaviours such as impulsivity. That's the same impulsivity that leads some Parkies to make expensive impulse purchases to the detriment of their bank balance (such as buying a Jaguar, says Claire beside me). Novelty seeking behaviour is another part of that spectrum, a psychobiological range that encompasses drug abuse too. Don't get me wrong -- I'm not suggesting that one Between the Sheets at the office party will send you on a downward spiral toward drug abuse any more than a single cigarette would lead inevitably to rolling spliffs the size of intercontinental ballistic missiles. It's never that simple.

But dopamine is a two-faced beast. One face smiles as we loosen up in the mornings, life gradually seeping into our stiff fingers as we fiddle with buttons. Smiles as we stretch and pull on socks. Smiles as our drugs bring us to life each day. The other face sneers as we spend mindless waking hours on the Internet or circling inessential nonsense in mail order catalogues. Or frittering away our money on lottery tickets and scratchcards. Dopamine is your best friend and your worst enemy. Dopamine is you at your best, on top of your game, blazing with imagination and enthusiasm. And dopamine is you at your worst, sick, skint and sorrowful. Dopamine will buoy you up and let you down. Dopamine will share the good times and the bad.

Dopamine has been at the heart of all anti-Parkinson's drug treatments for forty years. Drugs which boost or mimic dopamine are still all we have. To have dopamine as our best friend, we have to put up with its abuses.

It's time we had other molecules and drugs to unlock our stiff bodies. Other drugs to still our shakes. Other drugs to jumpstart our motionless selves. I want to be able to say no to dopamine. I want other friends to play with.

And I want to be able to say no to cocktails with stupid names.

TUMBLE
Monday, 10 January 2011

Upstairs in my home office. I pressed "save" on the document and switched on the answering machine. Three o'clock in the afternoon and time for a cup of tea. Earl Grey or Lapsang Souchong?

One second I was at the top of the stairs, the next I was at the bottom in a heap hitting the ground with the kind of seismic force associated with extinction of the dinosaurs. I've never seen the dog move so fast. There was a sickening crunch -- that's the only word for it -- as I landed on my ankle and it twisted. I resisted my instinct to get up immediately and instead lay on the floor to collect myself and perform an ad hoc inventory of the damage. I hadn't banged my head which was at least a start even if they were twinges of pain from other places. I had full rotation in my neck too. So far so good -- at least the command module was intact. My shoulder ached but appeared to have full mobility. The same for my ribs, pelvis and hips.

But all of this was no more than diversionary behaviour. A way of delaying the inevitable. The searing pain from my ankle left me in no doubt that I had done serious damage. Without even moving my foot, it was obviously in a poor way. Lying on my side I cautiously lifted the trouser leg. The ankle was enormous, swollen, with the taut skin of a Taiko drum. It reminded me of a pig's trotter. So much so that I burst out laughing. My foot seemed to belong to someone else, or something else. Still laughing at the absurdity of it, I prodded it with my finger. A mistake. Although I was alone in the house, I remember saying aloud "Ooh, that really hurts". I think I may, just possibly, have added a few other more vivid nouns and adjectives to the sentence.

I was certain it was broken.

All of which led me to the next issue. I was alone, lying on the floor, and unable to get to my feet. I needed to call for help. But the house phone was on top of the bookcase and my mobile was upstairs. And who would I call anyway? 999 was out of the question -- it wasn't actually life-threatening. Claire was at work in London and the children were in school. I dragged myself back upstairs, managed to knock my phone on to the floor where I could use it, and called Freia to say I needed to ask a favour. "I'm just in the car driving home" she said, before I had a chance to explain. "I'll call you back when I get home in a minute or two." After fifteen minutes, I called her. "It must be a big favour" she said. The moment I started to explain,

Freia interrupted "I'm on my way". Ten minutes later I was standing at the counter in Casualty.

Unless you are brought into hospital unconscious, the sequence of events at my local hospital is this. Before you see anybody medical, the receptionists first need to register you on "The System" -- name, date of birth, GP, and so on. Mostly logical but time-consuming questions. By this stage, the analgesia that comes from shock was wearing off and I was becoming a might tetchy. The question about food allergies tipped me over. "Any chance I could just see a doctor?" I said "I'm not planning to stay for dinner. And you can hold the wine list". She gave me one of those weary looks that suggested I was being neither big nor clever. More to the point, she would not be thwarted in her quest for information. We moved swiftly from food allergies to details of my next of kin and my religion. "Things that bad, huh?" I said "Would you like my choice of wood for my coffin?" We were evidently not going to be friends. She peeled off a label with what appeared to be a barcode and attached it to a printout of my notes. "Buy one get one free?" I enquired.

"And what appears to be the problem?" she eventually asked, having filled out the form to her satisfaction. "I think I have broken my ankle" I explained. "Why didn't you say earlier?" she replied. "Must have slipped my mind" I said. Suddenly a wheelchair mysteriously materialised and I was whisked off to X-ray by a huge Puerto Rican orderly. Neither ceremony nor explanation, but a lead blanket over my dangly bits. The radiographer, laughing, said he was on his break but he would take a quick snap of my ankle. His assistant, a trainee, asked whether she should have a crack at it. They both laughed. I managed a smile. Those long winter evenings must just fly past.

Somehow the presence of a wheelchair turns its occupant from human being to baggage, I thought as I was parked facing a wall in the fracture clinic to await the result. I felt as though I was being sent to the corner. "Looks like you got away with it" said the nurse, as though I had been base jumping or paragliding. No break, just ligament tears and bruising. No plaster cast, no strapping, just a leaflet of exercises. I wasn't sure whether to feel cheerful or cheated. Pablo the orderly parked me and my wheelchair back in reception. "How did it go?" asked the receptionist. I was touched by her interest. "Just a sprain" I replied. "Oh good" she said with an Ann Robinson wink "because we need your wheelchair".

I half expected her to say "you are the weakest link, goodbye!"

OFF PISTE COOKERY
Sunday 16 January 2011

It all happened so quickly that two thoughts went through my mind at the same time. Firstly that the flames from the pan were now engulfing the cooker hood and secondly, that a few seconds earlier, I had reassured the owner of the kitchen that there was no cause for concern -- I was a master of this kind of cookery and, in any case, bananas flambéed in rum was my signature dish. JR, whose house it was, reached a wholly different conclusion. After an instantaneous risk assessment, eloquently condensed to the name of our Saviour, shrieked at the top of his voice, he dashed for a fire extinguisher, giving me a few seconds to assess the damage. Certainly the dessert was a write-off. Even with my relatively cavalier approach to cookery, I recognised that carbon granules and plastic fragments from the cooker hood could not be passed off as an integral part of the dish. Or any dish. Secondly, and by the same token, the cooker hood had 'insurance claim' written all over it. Along with the frying pan for that matter, which had probably seen its last Full English. Affecting an air of nonchalance as JR returned with a fire blanket, I offered to knock up a fruit salad as an alternative to the Caribbean funeral pyre currently filling the space formerly occupied by his cooker.

That was more than thirty years ago but it's the kind of event that sticks in your mind. It was a valuable lesson for me and a timely reminder that one should never become overconfident in the kitchen. Of course JR also learned a valuable lesson -- never allow Jon to cook any dish involving fire when he has already sunk the best part of half a bottle of Scotch. This is, in the words of fire prevention officers, "an accident waiting to happen".

"And this would never have happened if you had stuck to the recipe" said JR. Barely discernible across a kitchen full of smoke, it didn't seem the right moment to say that there was no recipe, just a handful of ingredients and some drunkenly fertile culinary imagination.

But that's the thing with cooking. Over the intervening years I've come to realise that there are basically two types of cook -- for want of a better description I will call them scientists and artists. Let me explain.

The scientists will follow a recipe down to the last detail and by the end of their work, the result will look pretty much exactly like the picture in the cookbook. This is planned, methodical cooking for methodical planners. Delia Smith cookery. Unflustered, precise and correct. Vaguely Teutonic. The scientists will lay out every ingredient before beginning to cook. Nothing is left to chance. If a recipe calls for a dozen cardamom pods, the scientists will choose twelve of the most representative, the most typical, pods. If the recipe says 150 g of butter, it will get exactly that -- not 149 g, not 151 g. 210°C means 210°C. Neither 205°C nor 215°C. Everything is in grams and millilitres, not even ounces and fluid ounces. And nothing strikes more fear into the hearts of the scientist cook than recipes which need a 'glug' of oil, a 'handful' of lentils or a 'dollop' of cream.

This is more biochemistry than cooking, the work of the left brain, the logical and sensible, the structured and the cautious. Nothing is left to chance. And at the same time, nothing is left to the imagination. And there is no scope for creativity. A scientist, thumbing through a cookbook, finds a recipe needing 25g of vanilla sugar. He has no vanilla sugar. He has sugar and he has vanilla, but no vanilla sugar. He turns the page rather than make even this tiny logical connection. When he thinks of sugar, he thinks of the Krebs cycle not Sachertorte. His kitchen is a white, wipe down laboratory.

The artists, and despite my scientific background I number myself among them, have no truck with Delia and the biochemists. We will not be told how to cook. Recipe books full of weights, measures, temperatures and procedures make fingers fidget and eyes glaze over. The artist's kitchen is ramshackle, an impenetrable forest of gingham-lidded pickling jars, pots and pans. None of the crockery matches.

This is a Delia-free zone, with recipes on yellowed scraps of paper, or tucked away in drawers. Cookbooks have pictures of lavender bunches in Provence, mushrooms and truffles in the Perigord, strings of onions. Lifestyle books in essence. Nigella and Jamie country. Or Hugh Fearnley Whittingstall. Descriptions of fresh sardines, barbecued at the roadside in Portugal, hurried panini and espresso in Naples. Books that hint at recipes, suggest ideas and fire the imagination. Books to stir the dormant inner cooking god and send a shudder down the spine of the biochemists.

Like every other former student in Britain, I left university with a degree and a small but reliable repertoire of dishes -- spaghetti Bolognese, chilli con carne, and shepherd's pie. With a library of three recipes to draw upon, I swiftly calculated that, unless things changed, I could bank on eating shepherd's pie over six thousand times during my life, a daunting prospect even for the recipe's most passionate advocates.

I had a simple choice -- I could either learn more recipes or create more recipes. And in 1980, cookbooks were dull and prescriptive. People still remembered Fanny Craddock and the Galloping Gourmet. Dull, mainstream grey cookery. Post-war austerity cooking.

Then, like a punk rocker, came Keith Floyd, glass of wine in hand. This was my kind of cookery -- a handful of ingredients, a glug of imagination and a sprinkling of risk. No recipes, just a chance to run amok with flavours. And, inspired by Floyd's example, run amok I did. Nothing was out of bounds.

When I shared a flat near Paddington with my brother Charlie, in the 1980s, round the corner from a European delicatessen, I created meals that would have had Escoffier weeping into his cognac. Recipes that would make Mrs Beeton blub into her beetroot salad. Recipes for the ox like constitution of a starving Hemingway. Because for every triumph there was a failure. For each baked pear and peach brioche, there was a pig's liver biriani. Each pepper and macadamia pesto was offset by fennel and anchovy fritters. For every deep-fried camembert with gooseberry preserve, there was a calamari and cranberry crumble. For every plate licking triumph, there would be an abject culinary disaster. It was cooking that veered between success and failure. Food that stuck in your mind or in your gullet. Food that rode the ragged edge of disaster.

Those days seem a lifetime away. It doesn't take many untouched meals, each of them silent accusations of failure, to realise that children are the most conservative diners in the universe, and there is a limit to how many recipes you can create solely from ketchup. Besides, tremors and sharp knives do not mix well. There comes a point when self-preservation is more important.

But in my dreams, I am back in the Paddington flat, in the kitchen creating new recipes for that cookbook that I will probably never write. Seared duck fillets with panfried plantain, anyone? Maybe even flambéed in rum.

On second thoughts, maybe not.

INCREASINGLY SINISTER
Saturday 22 January 2011

John Sharp was a boy who could do anything. At eleven, he was already the tallest boy in the school, captain of the school football team, long jump record holder, played the trombone, a popular prefect and consistently top of the class. Predictably I admired and hated him in about equal degree. But more than any of these characteristics, he had a trump card -- he was ambidextrous. In exams, as one hand tired, he would simply switch to the other. No writer's cramp for him, just page upon page of clearly written answers. As the rest of us massaged our cramping claws like Peter Lorre in "The Hand", it didn't seem fair.

As the Parkinsonian tremors make writing anything a challenge, let alone exam essays, I am reminded of John Sharp. Not because of his capacity to write extensively but because I am gradually becoming ambidextrous in a manner of speaking. I wish I could say this was a deliberate or welcome change but in actual fact it's nothing more than another little adaptation on the Parkinson's journey. And we Parkies know a lot about adaptations.

Like most people, my Parkinson's is right side dominant, as one might expect from a right-hander. But in terms of pathology the right hand side leads the way for the left-hand side to follow reluctantly. So the state of my right hand side gives me a sneak preview of my left hand side in about six months time.

My right hand now has such a strong tremor that it doesn't so much shake as flap on bad days. I look like a penguin trying to fly. This turns typing into a linguistic form of Russian roulette. As many readers will doubtless have guessed, I use voice recognition software these days to compensate for this. Even that is not without its idiosyncrasies – 'To be or not to be' can only too easily become 'Two bee ore knot too B'. Of course typing is only one of life's many daily disciplines that are compromised by my seal fin flap. Such as eating and drinking. Soup is tackled only with extreme trepidation and even simple tasks like getting a glass of wine to my lips are close to impossible. What started initially as a resting tremor now has a degree of intention tremor as well. Or put another way, when I move my hand it no longer stops the tremor, which was always the case up to this point. A bit frustrating to be honest.

So the solution, well for the next six months or so, is to swap hands. When the right hand shakes, I type with the left. All glasses of wine are now held in the left hand. Soup spoons go straight to the left hand -- not worth even taking a chance with this one.

Of course this is not without its own issues. The left hand may shake less than the right, but it has always been less dextrous than the right too. How could it be otherwise -- the word dexterity comes from the Latin dexter, meaning right So for the moment it is Hobson's choice: a dextrous but flappy fin of a right hand or an untrained, if calmer, left hand. But for the moment I'm ambidextrous, even if not in the way I would have chosen. When the cricket season arrives, I shall probably bat left-handed. It can't be any worse than my right-handed batting.

Approximately ten percent of people are left-handed. So few that the Latin word for left -- sinister -- has acquired darker overtones. In many cultures left-handers are regarded as witches. The figurehead of the Cutty Sark is of a left-handed witch. The Ancient Zuni tribe, by comparison, regarded lefties as wiser and luckier. Unlike Joan of Arc, who was doubly unlucky -- burnt at the stake and, in all probability actually a right-hander but depicted as a lefty to reinforce the charge of witchcraft.

Such prejudices prevail into recent history. My mother, a left-hander born in a barely more enlightened age, was made to write with her right hand at school, the left-hand even tied to her side in order to prevent its surreptitious usage. A practice and prejudice that seems both comical and tragic. If this were 1690s Salem, it would be believable, but this was Wigan in the 1930s.

Mmmm -- maybe you're right.

On the whole we live in a right-handed world. Especially so in Britain. We drive our cars from the right-hand seat. This evolved to allow riders to use the whip in the right-hand to fend off other road users. Even road rage is right-handed.

Mice (that's computer mice, not the squeaky cheese eaters), golf clubs, calligraphy pens, and so on are all made for the right-hand. The kitchen is an even more dextrophilic environment. Take corkscrews for instance -- designed for the right-handed tippler. The lefty imbiber, struggling with the thread, remained parched just that little bit longer. Elsewhere the hazards mount up. Bread knives, scissors, milk saucepans -- all sharp or dangerous and all designed for the dexter rather the sinister amongst us. So it come as no surprise to you to learn not only that the life expectancy of lefties is marginally less than that of right-handed people, but that most of the difference is the result of domestic accidents. Sharp blades and boiling liquids mean there are greater tribulations for the left-hander than a relative inability to open a bottle of Chardonnay.

So for the moment, like John Sharp, I'm ambidextrous. Not ambidextrous in the classical understanding of the word, but ambidextrous in my own way -- a ham-fisted, quivering, clumsy and useless way. But it's just a phase.

Before long I will be really sinister...

UNEASY RIDER
Unpublished – January 2011

Whilst the amalgamation of the bicycle and the internal combustion engine might seem to most to be a marriage made in heaven, that was not the case in my parents' house. Not for my father the liberation of the open road, the wind and sun on your face. My father had trenchant views on motorbikes and, as a doctor, regarded motorcyclists as little more than organ donors still on the hoof so to speak. Motorbikes, in turn, he considered to be a needlessly elaborate means of committing suicide. Testing the water, my brother Charlie, seventeen at the time, once incautiously expressed a desire to buy a motorbike. My father lowered his newspaper and, peering over the top of his reading glasses, said "Why don't I just buy you a gun?"

Besides, my father had been a little less than impressed with my own motorcycling exploits. Well I say motorcycling but that's perhaps overegging the pudding. Let me explain. At my university, all freshers were given a room on campus, ostensibly to ease assimilation into the university. However my second year at university meant that I had to find digs in town. The university itself was approximately 3 miles out of the city centre at the top of a long steep hill. Nobody walked. Most students used the bus. Others had smoky and unreliable cars. A small insular handful of grease monkeys had motorcycles which they parked in the service road beneath 5W. When they weren't in lectures, which appeared to be all the time, the riders could be found beside their machines, tinkering with spanners and wrenches or polishing chrome. Like a flange of gorillas, the young males revved their engines for attention. Top of the pack, like a dominant male silverback, was Steve, vaguely reminiscent of Jim Morrison in leathers. He had a Triumph Bonneville and a girlfriend who was the spitting image of Julia Roberts.

Was I envious? If you can imagine the green of tree frogs, of emeralds, of rainforests, of ripe tropical limes, you're on the right lines. I was greener than the greenest green thing with envy. It was clear -- motorbikes impressed girls. And the better the motorbike the more impressed and impressive the girl.

I decided my days of public transport were over. Why should I stand, teeth chattering, in the queue for the bus, when I could be snarling my way into the sunset with Julia Roberts riding pillion. It was time to buy a motorbike, and a powerful one at that. A brilliant plan except for one tiny detail -- being penniless, like most students, it called for an approach to the Bank of Dad. The question was how best to sell the idea of a motorbike to my father – a practical and sensible necessity was probably the better tack than babe magnet. In any case, he wasn't ready for a Hollywood actress as a daughter-in-law. Save that till later, I thought.

My father's response was predictably tepid. Largely unconvinced, he grudgingly conceded that independence from public transport was at least a laudable objective and that some sort of two wheeled flirtation with the internal combustion engine had a certain logic. Of course I should have quit while I was ahead, nodding approval at his appraisal and casually suggesting some numbers he might like to use when writing the cheque. That would have been sensible. Less sensible was trying to seal the deal with an ejaculatory request for a 500cc Kawasaki.

Even after drawing attention to the fact that I had not passed my test and could therefore drive nothing larger than 250cc bike, he made it clear that I wouldn't even reach that capacity ceiling. No, he felt that a 50cc moped would more than adequately fulfil my transport requirements. I was deflated.

Did I say deflated? Deflated in the sense that the Hindenburg was deflated in 1937. That deflated. It was just as well that my leathers were on sale or return. A moped for goodness sake. Julia Roberts went up in a puff of smoke. My motorcycling days were over before they had begun. One minute it was all Top Gun and Kelly Le Brock, the next it was Last of the Summer Wine with Nora Batty in a sidecar.

I did my best to appear interested when my father arrived home with the moped. I can't even remember what make it was - a phenomenon known to psychiatrists as post-traumatic amnesia. The brain blocks out things too uncomfortable to remember. I do remember however that it had a top speed of around 40, presumably downhill with a hurricane behind it. Going uphill, even this searing pace was unattainable. Joggers overtook me. Schoolchildren laughed. Even babies pointed. Lorries seemed to take a particular pleasure in forcing me into the gutter, where doubtless they felt I belonged. A one-legged unicyclist could have gone quicker. What should have been the thunderous, throbbing roar of the Kawasaki was replaced by a sound like a guinea pig breaking wind.

Anonymity was the order of the day. Anything to make myself invisible. I toyed briefly with the idea of some kind of disguise, perhaps a false moustache, and a change of clothes. But then I looked like a French onion seller. More rather than less conspicuous. Even my friends called me Compo.

When I had reached the end of my tether with this style cramping, ego crushing, ridiculous mechanical fartwheel, fate intervened. Daydreaming after lectures, rather than paying attention to the road, I misjudged a corner and clipped the kerb. The moped went one way, I went another, mercifully landing next to (rather than in) an ornamental gorse bush. My trousers were torn, I had grazed my knee and bent both arms of my spectacles. And to add insult to injury, my fountain pen had leaked.

You couldn't even injure yourself properly on a moped.

"Are you okay?" asked a female voice as I sat up and picked grass out of my glasses. I assured her I was fine. She waited a minute while I regained my composure, if not my credibility.

"I think your bike is broken" she said. The moped, resting against a lamppost, was leaking oil and its front wheel was buckled.

"Good" I said "in fact very good". Sometimes God smiles.

SHIPBUILDING PT 1-30 YEARS AGO
Wednesday 26th January 2011

Some thirty years ago, before I had even started to do research on Parkinson's, let alone acquired the condition, I bought a ship model kit in a small shop in Greenwich. Let me explain. I had just spent the morning viewing the Cutty Sark followed, after a liquid lunch, by an afternoon at the National Maritime Museum admiring its many beautiful shipyard models. Saturated by this immersion in nauticalia, it seemed natural to want to build my own ship. For those interested, it was Billing Boats catalogue number 415.

This was not entirely an unprecedented leap of faith. I had built more than my share of plastic models over the years, my bedroom bookshelves groaning with endless Spitfires and Hurricanes, to the exasperation of our cleaner, Mrs Gossett. Barely a day went by without one or other model losing propellor blades, tailfins, radio aerials or undercarriage as Mrs Gossett dusted my aircraft collection with all the tenderness of the Luftwaffe. Inevitably, my First World War boxkite-flimsy biplanes and triplanes suffered worst as Baron von Gossett scythed through squadron after squadron of Sopwith Camels. Indeed, like the Forth Bridge, maintenance of this collection of military aviation was a constant undertaking.

So, in model-making terms I had previous, so to speak. But bizarrely, among the many aeroplanes were but a tiny handful of ships, mostly warships and mostly German -- the Royal Navy seem to have little to compare with the Bismarck, Scharnhorst, Prinz Eugen or Graf Spee. In general these had been hastily assembled and poorly finished. I was far too impatient ever to follow instructions, and found painting the models a chore akin to washing up after Sunday lunch.

So, with an impatient nature and tendency to overlook critical detail, what possessed me in my early twenties to take on a huge wooden model? Instead of a set of neatly formed plastic pieces, here were sheets of wood, marked out but uncut. This was indubitably going to take more than a tube of polystyrene glue. Tools were required, tools with names I'd never heard before. And there were so many pieces. Even by Billings standards, this was considered an 'advanced' kit. The kind of kit you would attempt only after several easier models. Not a first kit. But in those days, I was immortal. I could do anything. I would not be put off by such hollow advice. Sure I could make it.

What I didn't consider was time. And as a postgraduate student, free time is at a premium. A cursory examination of the instruction booklet and its estimated time frame led me to wonder if I was building a model or the actual ship.

I procrastinated endlessly until, in 1984, after opening the box and lovingly poring over its contents one last time, I realised I was not going to make the model. But having spent some £50 or so on it, at that time a reckless sum of money for a PhD student, nor was I going to throw it away. So it went in the loft of the flat. Then when I married, it went in the loft of our house. And when we had children, it went in the loft of the new house. In its original packaging, a damning indictment of my squandering youth. Forgotten. But unforgiven.

And there it lay, untouched for the last twenty five years. Until a month ago, when looking for old mortgage documents, I came across a large dusty box. I rubbed the dust aside and there it was -- Billing Boats catalogue number 415 "Danmark". The box had been gnawed by mice. Probably several generations of mice. By the flickering light of a failing torch, I opened the cardboard case. Inside it was pristine. Every last piece was there, exactly as I had packaged it up a quarter of a century earlier, in sullen admission of defeat.

And as I sat there in the cold loft, a thought entered my mind. A stupid thought. An irrational, futile thought. The kit was intact in every respect the same as the day, thirty years ago when I bought it in Greenwich. It could still be made into a viable ship model.

I could make it.

But if I had been beaten by this model before, when fit and healthy, how would I fare now? How would I piece together the miles of rigging, tying those tiny little knots with hands that cannot hold a soup spoon still. Like I said, a stupid idea.

But the more I tried to put the idea to the back of my mind, the more it resisted. Only when I spoke to a Swedish rigger, was I persuaded.

Parkinson's is all about challenges. And for each of us our challenges differ. For some, it is the running of marathons. For others, it is fundraising, cooking, cycling or any one of a million other challenges. Perhaps it is our way of saying to the Parkinson's "is that your best shot?" when we all know that it isn't. But still we all, in our own ways, rant and rage against the dying of the light.

My challenge is no different. The world will not be a better place if I finish the model or if I don't. The sun will still rise. Nobody will be richer or poorer. It will not cure disease or rid the world of famine. In short it will make no difference to anybody except myself.

But build it I will.

And I will keep you all updated on my progress (not every week mind you). And I will tell you about the ship and its history while I build it. You will be my safety net ensuring that I don't find I have "been too busy" or "couldn't be bothered" or "was too tired". It may be difficult. In fact I would be disappointed if it wasn't. But maybe, just maybe, one day years from now, somebody will admire the ship and Alex will say "my dad made that and, you know the remarkable bit, he had Parkinson's".

February

Do not go gentle into that good night,
Old age should burn and rave at close of day;
Rage, rage against the dying of the light.

Dylan Thomas (1914-1953)

THE VOICE OF EXPERIENCE
Tuesday 1st February 2011

Experience was never good. Experience was the word our parents used to describe the things that were not good. Falling face first into stinging nettles was an experience. Working half the night to finish your geography homework and still getting a D was an experience. Seeing your sweetheart kissing Christopher Bowles behind the bike sheds was an experience (and he had spots too!).

As I grew older, experience took on a different meaning. It became something to put on my CV, something that would help me get to the interview, something to swing that first job. It was something precious, at a premium somehow, scarce as hen's teeth. Experience set you apart from the other candidates at the job interview. My sandwich year at university was an experience, though I knew it not at the time. It became my experience on my CV.

Into middle age, and experience became something else again. In fact it became one word with age, as in ageandexperience. It was impossible to have one without the other. If you were old, then by default you had experience. And by the same token, if you had experience, you must be old. I relished both, acknowledging the ultimate triumph of cunning and guile over youth and exuberance. "Age before beauty" giggle a group of teenage girls theatrically opening a door for old Mr Shakyshuffles."Pearls before swine" I mutter with rictus smile.

But now we have a new form of 'experience'. We no longer shop -- we have a 'shopping experience'. Holidays in Spain are 'sun, sea and Sangria experiences. Car salesmen invite us to 'experience' the latest Jaguar - not drive it you understand but immerse ourselves in the experience. When we are taken ill, we do not go on a blue flash dash to hospital - we have an 'acute healthcare experience'. We no longer eat in a restaurant -- no, it's an experience we are apparently crying out for.

Take this Tuesday, when I am greeted by a waitress who is at pains to tell me she is called Tammy and that she and her pearly white teeth are charged with the task of ensuring that my dining experience lives up to my expectations. I am at a loss to know where to start. I have only stopped by for a pie and a pint. Enjoyable though it will likely be, I'm not expecting 'an experience'. No choirs of angels, no dancing girls, no Jimi Hendrix album -- in fact, nothing short of transubstantiation that will distinguish it from a steak and kidney pie and a glass of best bitter. I ask Tammy what my expectations should be, so that I will know instantly if my pie falls short of 'an experience'. Tammy is clearly used to this, places a menu in front of me and skates away. Did I mention that she was on roller skates? Half an hour later, she leaves the bill and mechanically asks me how the food was. "An experience" I reply. It is only when she returns a minute later with the manager that I realise that Tammy has misunderstood. In any case, it's impossible to keep a straight face when talking to a man wearing a suit and roller skates.

Experiences are everywhere. Only yesterday a letter arrived from my bank. Nothing unusual about that -- I get plenty of letters from them, mostly offering loans, credit transfers, ISAs, insurance and so on. Or reiterating my overdraft terms in starchy prose that makes me think of big dogs with sharp teeth. All the sort of stuff that bank managers get their knickers in a twist about. The letter began "important changes -- please read". Normally this means the opposite -- the letters go straight in the shredder, to be transmogrified into bedding for the guinea pigs. But this letter was different. Such is my exalted standing with the bank that I now have a 'personal banking adviser' who, if the letter was to be believed, lived only to enhance my 'banking experience'. Nothing was too much trouble.

Well call me an old curmudgeon if you will, but my idea of a banking experience is probably very different from his. Lights, music and the chorus line from the Folies Bergere in my local branch would perhaps constitute an experience. A computer glitch transferring the assets of a large multinational to my current account would constitute an experience. On the other hand a free ballpoint pen, a different coloured cheque-book and a logo-emblazoned diary do not make me think I'm special. Nor for that matter, did misspelling my name.

I can hardly wait for my next neurology appointment "Hi, I'm Dr_____. I'm your neurologist today and I look forward to making your Parkinson's experience the best it can be."

'OK cure me' I shall say.

'Oh, and put the rollerskates away'

DRAGON TAMING
Sunday 6th February 2011

People keep some strange pets. Every once in a while, the redtops will spawn a news story along the lines of "Man Kept Python in Bedsitter" or "Neighbour's Cheetah Ate My Pekinese", highlighting the perils of keeping large exotic animals in inappropriately small dwellings. Often it is the owners who seem to be the problem. You always have to worry about the kind of people who keep large slavering dogs with names like Satan, Thor or Killer in Hackney flats. Dogs with spiky collars and leads made of the kind of chain used to anchor large warships. As a rule large slavering dogs tend to have large slavering owners.

But for many people with Parkinson's, pets are a source of companionship as well as providing a stimulus to exercise. Perhaps not Thor or Killer but small dogs, for example, seem sensible. Or a cat. But for those of us with the limited mobility that Parkinson's so generously provides, a dragon might seem an ill-advised choice. Keeping large predatory animals in a domestic scenario is, for many, a recipe for disaster. And even with the current passion for exotica, there is no escaping the fact that a dragon requires careful handling. If you're the kind of person who worries that their pet Jack Russell might take a nip at the postman, this is not, on the face of it, a choice of animal that leaps out at you. Except literally.

But for many people with Parkinson's, a dragon is paradoxically an ideal companion. I bought my dragon a little over a year ago and I have to say it's changed my life. You can obtain dragons from many suppliers, but I do advise you to pick a reputable dealer with an appropriate returns policy. Dragons are not for everyone.

I should say upfront that my dragon is much more than a pet. I expect it to work hard for me, making life easier at home and at work. I expect it to obey commands without question. I expect it to obey first-time and to perform the requested tasks quickly, efficiently and with good grace. For the most part it does.

The key to it all is training. Just as with cats and dogs, so it is with dragons. A large puppy, left untrained, quickly becomes a large untrained and uncontrollable dog. And it's exactly the same with dragons. It's important be firm with them from the outset. The dragon needs to know who is the boss. If you are to be responsible dragon owner, you should start the training as soon as the dragon is out of its box. Give it a few basic commands. Let it adjust to the sound of your voice and the way you speak. This is particularly important because dragons fix on one voice in the same way that babies imprint on their mothers.

Read to the dragon. Once the dragon has adjusted to the sound of your voice and recognises you as its master, there is nothing it will enjoy more than a bedtime story. You can read Alice in Wonderland, President Kennedy's inaugural address or whatever. It doesn't matter. The dragon loves the sound of your voice. And the more you read to the dragon, the more the dragon respects your authority.

And don't be afraid to use a trained dragon in the workplace. I have just started a new job, and my employers have provided a very helpful work dragon. A fine beast, quick and responsive. I've not finished its training yet but already it is keen to help.

I suppose I should come clean at this point and explain the previous few paragraphs. Many of my Parkie friends will know exactly what I'm talking about. Others may think that I have lost my ability to distinguish between reality and fantasy. Not so. Or that these are the first insidious steps on the path to dementia. Again no. Or perhaps some may think that I am encouraging irresponsible pet ownership or in some way tempting people into purchasing giant lizards. Still no.

But this is really the point at which I have to break (or at least bend) my "no advertising or endorsements" rule and say that the dragon I'm talking about is Dragon NaturallySpeaking, the voice recognition software package popular amongst people with Parkinson's. Suddenly the first few paragraphs make sense, yes?

Like many people with Parkinson's, I find typing challenging, slow and inaccurate. My fingers stumble, lurch and sprawl across the keyboard, like a hen party emerging from a Basildon nightclub. A page of text will take me a morning by conventional typing. It takes a tenth of that by dictation. Voice recognition software allows me to write letters to friends who haven't received one from me in ages. Voice recognition software allows me to write this blog. Voice recognition software keeps me in gainful employment where otherwise I might have faltered.

Of course voice recognition has been around for awhile and dragons are not the only animals with this power. Parrots learn to mimic the human voice with surprising accuracy although they can't yet write a blog and they are rubbish at Scrabble. And on the subject of parrots, albeit after one of my feebler links, let me end with a joke I heard told by Barry Cryer on Radio 4 a week or so back.

A woman goes into a pet shop looking to buy a parrot and sees a beautiful grey African parrot priced at £20. She asks the shop owner why the parrot is so cheap. The shopkeeper explains it's cheap because the parrot used to live in a brothel, and its language might be a bit fruity. Still it is a bargain so the woman says "I'll take him" and pays the £20.

She takes the parrot home and uncovers the cage. The parrot looks at her and squawks "new madam -- nice".

Then the woman's two daughters walk in. 'New girls, too' says the parrot. 'Very nice!'

Then her husband arrives.

'Hello, Keith,' says the parrot.

SHIPBUILDING PT 2:
SOME GROUND RULES
Sunday 13th February 2011

I've started building the model of the Danmark and already I have been struck by the parallels between model building and Parkinson's. Firstly there's no denying the fact that model builders are almost by definition obsessive. Who else but an obsessive would consider spending so much time on what is, to all intents and purposes, a completely fruitless exercise. Only an obsessive would fret over tiny irrelevant details, agonising over the exact shade of white that a Danish training ship from the 1930s would typically be. Or whether the ship should be portrayed in port or under full sail. Decisions decisions decisions.

People with Parkinson's know plenty about obsession. Partly, it's our personae. A tendency to be introspective and obsessive perhaps. And when you add some of the drugs we take, the results can, let's face it, be rather unbecoming. The dopamine agonists (and I'm not going to name them -- you know who they are) are rightly or wrongly notorious for their ability to promote obsessional behaviour. You know the kind of thing -- whole days spent on Facebook, credit card meltdown on Amazon, endlessly organising and reorganising one's bookshelves or even spending hour after hour piecing together several hundred pieces of wood to make a model boat. To prove what?

Insight is everything. At least I recognise the signs of obsession. As it is with alcoholism, recognition is the first step to control. And it has taken a model of a Danish training ship to point it out. So having spotted the enemy so to speak, what next? Well it's all about setting limits, so my solution will be to allocate a specific time to work on the model, not allowing the elastic nature of the task to dominate. I will break it down into a series of small objectives, each attainable within say a lunch hour. As they say, the longest journey starts with a single step.

So recognising obsession is life lesson 1.

Lesson 2 is about limitations and knowing them for what they are. Sure we can rail against them in our frustration but we do better when we learn to work within our limitations or to find ways round them. Sometimes the direct route to the destination is best. Other times it isn't. Sometimes the journey is quicker alone, sometimes one needs company. The obsessional me would eschew all help, in the belief that any assistance would somehow nullify the task or would render it meaningless. As though it was cheating in some way.

The realist in me takes a more pragmatic view. There is no doubt in my mind that assistance will be required making this model. The same assistance that will be needed as this condition progresses. But how do you break a lifetime's habit of self-sufficiency? How do you first say "I need help here"? Perhaps asking for help with the model will make it easier for me to ask for help in other areas. Perhaps that's how you start -- by asking for help on a small thing. Perhaps by asking for help on small matters, one is really secretly asking for help on the bigger things. Lesson 2 is learning to ask for help. Help with the model and help with the Parkinson's.

Life lesson 2 is to learn to ask for help.

The third lesson is related and concerns instructions. The instructions in this kit are, as you might imagine, voluminous and prescriptive. Perfect for the able-bodied, rubbish for those with Parkinson's. Completely impossible to perform. So what do I do? Abandon the model in the sure and certain knowledge that I'm physically unable to make the intricate cuts and manipulations specified in the instructions. Again the Parkinson's comes to the rescue. If this condition teaches you nothing else, it is to find solutions. So following in the time-honoured tradition, let me say right now that I will take shortcuts. In the same way that I take shortcuts in my daily life, anything to make life more straightforward, I will do the same with this model. Sure, I'm looking to challenge myself with this model. But equally, I will not be dominated by it. I will not flounder. Instead I will ask for help and, as with the model, I will learn to do so with my Parkinson's. I will also, as in my daily living, learn to make efficient use of shortcuts. And above all, it will be fun.

So life lesson 3 is to look for shortcuts to make life easier.

I will not be obsessive. I will ask for help. I will take shortcuts. These are not admissions of defeat but the roadmap to victory.

PERFECT SUNDAY
Wednesday 16th February 2011

For ten years, the 1980s, I shared a first-floor flat in Bayswater, that mini Mecca for backpackers, holidaymakers and artists. Beneath the flat, in a faded Regency terrace, was a television repair shop, run by an East End wideboy, the spitting image of Michael Elphick. His business partner, a stubbly dishevelled Greek in sandals and torn cardigan, chain-smoked when he wasn't hacking his lungs up. The stale reek of the shop's fetid air, a toxic mix of sweat, old tobacco and solder was enough to make you blink. Charlie said it was an opium den. In the decade I lived there, I recall hardly any customers in the shop.

Across the road was a pub. Once a self-satisfied Watney's crimson with velvet plush booth seats, brass tables and polished copper finials, then suddenly stripped overnight to bare wood and sawdust in ersatz Georgian rustic chic after an inexplicable stylistic diktat from the brewers. It didn't matter -- drinkers came and went, seemingly younger with each passing year. And always from the other side of the world. Like some strange outpost of Earls Court, the summer nights echoed to garrulous Australian laughter and clipped Afrikaner vowels as patrons spilled out onto the pavement. An off-licence further up the street stocked South African wines long before they were fashionable.

Next door was a launderette run, as was the adjacent shop, by an ever-changing extended Indian family. To this day I don't know who was related to whom. They sold everything from yoyoes to yak cheese, from samosas to steak knives, from biros to bubblegum. And if they didn't sell it, they knew someone who did. The shop, launderette and pub are still there.

At one end, the street opened onto a lawned square, shaded by mature plane trees with benches and a small central fountain. Each year in November the residents around the square lit candles, and shared their sparklers and fireworks. The loud bangs triggered car alarms.

Like fireworks, my perfect Sundays were always in November. Surprising perhaps that I should always prefer the crisp cold of a clear, bright November day, with its skeletal leafless trees. But autumn has always been my season. Often I would be working on Saturdays, writing or analysing data. Somehow the working week seemed to expand to fill the weekend. But Sundays were precious.

There is no greater feeling than drifting into consciousness gradually at ten o'clock rather than being clubbed awake at seven by an alarm clock louder than a Saturn V launch. And, for me, ten o'clock on a Sunday morning meant one place – Maison Bouquillon in Moscow Road, the best patisserie in west London at the time. Always packed at the weekends, Bouquillon made pastries to die for -- the best tarte aux fraises south of Hampstead and my own particular favourite, the Religieuse, a double chou filled with vanilla custard, in fanciful representation of the shape of a well rounded nun.

But Bouquillon was more than a patisserie, it was an institution. When threatened with closure by unsympathetic landlords, a petition garnered twenty eight thousand signatures. Fewer sought Nelson Mandela's release. The Sunday Times, a Religieuse and an espresso doppio, listening to the babble of Orthodox Greeks, French exchange students and Polish matrons was European cafe society at its best. I could have stayed all day.

Moscow Road led on to Queensway, and then, past a bratwurst stand, to Hyde Park, eyes half shut against the low winter sun with warm gloves, Doctor Who scarf and fireman's greatcoat keeping the cold at bay. A brisk stroll to the Serpentine, and a reflective half-hour crumbling the crusts of a loaf for the ducks. Then to Kensington Gardens and the Round Pond, where small children sailed model boats, their fathers peering anxiously at precious new yachts, fresh from Hamleys, becalmed in the middle.

From the Round Pond, along the Bayswater Road past railings heavy with paintings. Purple sunsets, African warriors painted on black velvet, improbably large breasted women and London scenes made entirely from clock parts jostle with "I (heart) London" T-shirts and plastic policeman's helmets. Past the bookshops and delicatessens of Notting Hill, then down Campden Hill Road to the Windsor Castle, with its beckoning wood fire and smells of home cooking. I'm surprised to discover that I'm hungry. I finish the colour supplement over a steak and kidney pie and a glass of best bitter. Ham and Rollo arrive and we talk about nothing and everything. More beer. We have no plans for the afternoon and decide, on a whim, to go to the V&A.

We amble erratically down Kensington Church Street with another favourite watering hole, the Churchill, then along Kensington High Street past the Albert Hall and down Exhibition Road to the V&A. Ham wants to see the Raphael cartoons, while I head for the William Morris exhibition. Rollo ducks out briefly to go and look at the dinosaurs in the Natural History Museum. He paces out the full length of the diplodocus and rejoins us at the V&A, to reassure us that the dinosaur has not changed in length since his last visit. The relief. To all parties. A cup of tea and a slice of lemon drizzle cake as the sun slips lower. I write postcards, buy books in the V&A shop and say my goodbyes.

The Christmas lights are bright along Kensington High Street. I stop to watch the sunset over the Serpentine, then back to the flat. A long soak in a hot bath, a glass of whisky and a chapter or two of The Life of Goya, while warming my toes by the fire. Even the pub is quiet.

I close the curtains. It has started to snow.

A NIGHT AT T'OPERA
Tuesday 22nd February 2011

When you've been going to the opera as long as I have, nigh on forty years, you notice a few things. The audience for one. Without hearing a note played, I reckon I could identify the composer clearly on the basis of the audience in the bar before the curtain rises. Assertive career women in suits? You're probably in for an evening of Bizet's Carmen. Lovey-dovey fortysomething couples sipping fizzy white wine suggests Puccini while the presence of down-at-heel corduroy intellectuals, copies of the Guardian underarm, signifies an evening of Mozart. And an aged audience, dressed almost entirely in black, grimly sipping their gin and tonics, can only mean one thing -- Wagner.

And the same differences prevail in the auditorium. Some fidget, some hum along and others sit stock still. Others, worst of all, talk. Yes, talk! To talk about the opera itself, although unacceptable, is the least understandable. But to discuss taramasalata recipes during the overture should carry a custodial sentence. I remember one woman reading a newspaper throughout the performance. And a broadsheet paper at that. Distracting? Just a tad. But nowhere near as distracting as the man, two seats along, who appeared to be changing a colostomy bag during The Marriage of Figaro in 1994. Or the coach party from Bletchley eating crisps during Tosca. I tell you flogging is too good. Claire says 'I don't know why you go to the opera. It only upsets you'.

She is right of course -- most opera plots are ridiculous when you stop to think about it and even the individual arias have daft titles. On the whole arias are known by their first line, and taken in isolation, seem banal. Mind you, when sung by inadequate singers, they really are banal. One 1982 rendition of *Questa o Quella* (this or that) specially transposed for a tone deaf baritone was emphatically neither this nor that. Nor anything really. Of course tenors are the worst. *Una furtiva lagrima (a secret tear)* in the hands of a particularly wobbly tenor will end in more than private sobbing. A performance in every sense of the word. It's just as well that Donizetti has been dead for some 200 years. Of course, if blubbing is your bag, nobody does it better than Puccini. Nearly all of his operas end in tragic but wholly predictable deaths. Even in his happier operas, and there are not many, the body count usually matches an average CSI episode.

Take *La Boheme*, the story of penniless artists living in a Parisian garret. When Mimi, the main love interest arrives, Rodolfo is gobsmacked and forgets his manners. *Que Gelida Manina* (your tiny hand is frozen) is a statement of the blindingly obvious. It's -10° outside and Mimi has tuberculosis but no gloves. Dimwit, quit singing and find her some gloves. Oh and put the kettle on. Two hours of warbling later, she is dead. A cup of Bovril might have given her at least a fighting chance.

Of course it would have taken more than a hot drink to save *Madam Butterfly*, the young geisha who marries an impulsive American naval officer in search of cheap thrills. In the second act, when she trills her way through *Un Bel di Vedremo* (one fine day), the audience knows very well that hubby is not going to return. No, he is shacked up with a floozy back home. And it all goes downhill from there. A double hanky weepie as my mother would say, in her own emotional Richter scale. And probably not a ringing endorsement of American foreign policy, if we're honest.

I can't hear *Nessun Dorma* (nobody is going to get a wink tonight) without thinking of Pavarotti and listening to the windows rattle as he hits the high notes at the end. And who could sleep through that? In Italy they sell alarm clocks which wake you to the strains of *Nessun Dorma*.

And when Lauretta dotingly sings *O Mio Babbino Caro* (O my beloved/extraordinarily gullible daddy) to her father Gianni Scicchi, he knows instantly that he is being set up for a major financial setback. What is it this time -- a pony? A car? This is the stuff of opera. No wonder that in Rigoletto, the tenor sings *La Donna É Mobile* (the woman is mobile). Upwardly mobile, I imagine. In Gotterdammerung, Brunnhilde sweeps Siegfried out of the house with the words *Zu Neuen Taten* (onward to great deeds) or put another way "will you just get out from under my feet". He's hardly gone before she's got her feet up in front of breakfast TV

Mind you, the chaps are wise to this sort of trick. *Wahn! Wahn! Überall Wahn!* (You're all potty, the lot of you) sings the cobbler Sachs, unimpressed with the youth of today -- well, fifteenth century Nuremberg anyway. And Puccini's hero Calaf does not have infinite patience and tells his servant *Non Piangere Liu* (just stop blubbing -- now. It's getting on my nerves). Even his dad Timor pitches in with *Per l'ultima Volta* (for the last time ... how many times do I have to go on repeating myself?)

Of course nowadays you don't need to know any Italian, German or French. Modern opera houses have surtitles projected above the stage. My friend Ham was decidedly unimpressed. "You know, Jon" he would say "I don't mind what language they sing, just so long as I don't understand it".

But even surtitles are no guarantee of understanding, as I found out years back watching Rheingold in Leeds at the Grand Theatre. In the adjacent seats were a ruddy Yorkshire farmer and his wife. As the curtain fell on the gods stealing the gold from the grubby dwarf Alberich, the farmer leant over and whispered to his wife "Aye, just proves it Marion -- where there's muck there's brass".

KEEPING UP APPEARANCES
Sunday 27th February 2011

Close friends know that I don't "do" fashion in any understanding of the word. Especially clothes. It means nothing to me. As far as I know, Karl Lagerfeld is a Bavarian brewery. Alexander McQueen - wasn't he a Manchester United centre half? And Gucci is a type of pasta, right? I'll have the Gucci carbonara please. And a bottle of Lagerfeld.

Alice despairs of me. This is a girl who knows her Coco Chanel from her Christian Lacroix, her Giorgio Armani from her Dolce and Gabbana. A Versace victim, a Prada fashionista, a Gaultier glamourpuss. In her hierarchy of fashion, I am on a par with an amoeba. A fashion vacuum. And she's right. Fashion means nothing to me. I buy clothes based on function. The principal function of a jumper, and forgive my naivete, seems to be to keep the wearer warm. It doesn't have to be any particular shape, colour or texture. It just has to be warm.

My great aunt Kath, a tiny sparrow of a woman with an unquenchable yen for knitting, is probably largely to blame. Throughout the latter part to my childhood and early twenties, I had a new jumper each Christmas from her. As did the entire family. From July each year, her living room echoed to the clickety-clack of knitting needles wielded with eyeblinking speed. And each Christmas morning there would be five parcels, labelled and wrapped in brown paper, waiting for us under the tree. So closely guarded was the secret that there was no way of predicting what you would find on opening the package. Well, it was a jumper, we knew that. Sometimes there would be a beautiful cream Arran weighing as much as a sheep. A jumper made to handle weather with a capital W. The kind of jumper built for shepherds tramping the Scottish moors in blizzards or for trawlermen in a force nine gale off Stornoway. A man's jumper.

Other years her magic fingers would conjure strange ringnecked pullovers in lime green or khaki, or one of those many shades of brown too anonymous even to merit a name. Wools that were somehow always in the Busy Bee's sale. The sight of my father, forcing an "it's just what I wanted" smile, while squeezing into a tank top the colour of budgie vomit is an image not easily erased.

Colours aside, these were woollies for the Yorkshire winter. Like dry stone walls in wool. And although Kath has been gone -- "called home" as she poetically called it -- more than twenty years ago, I still have one of her jumpers -- a simple plain round neck in a colour I can only describe as oxidised avocado. It's a little tight these days. The thirty-year-old Jon's bones were less amply fleshed than the fifty three-year-old model. Still, the added vents hardly show. Apart from the colour.

Talking of colours, answer me this. Why is it that, no matter what colour your jumper or how many days you wear it, it never seems to match the fluff in your navel? This bothers me. For that matter, why is earwax a different colour in each year?

Jumpers are one thing. What I don't wear are gilets, mankinis or any of a host of clothing items calculated to embarrass the wearer when looking through their family snaps in years to come. Like my flower power shirt with collars the size of elephant ears, bought in the optimistic aftermath of Woodstock. When it comes to fashion, I've learnt the hard way. So nowadays, I get dressed, that's all. Never really think about it. I don't make "style statements". Unless of course "Dishevelled " is the latest line from Vivienne Westwood. Actually it probably is so that's perhaps not a very good example. "Dishevelled -- the new black". But you get my point. If the Jon Stamford 2011 wardrobe has an air of familiarity about it, that's not surprising. It's the same as the 2010 wardrobe. In fact, except where clothes have worn out, it's largely unchanged from the last millennium.

I see this as a matter of pride not prejudice. So it pains me to say that things have got to change. And all because of the Parkinson's. When you draw attention to yourself unwittingly by your stumbling rigid walk and cocktail shaker arms, people inevitably take more notice of other aspects of your appearance. In anybody else, it matters not one jot. Nobody notices whether the able-bodied are wearing torn T-shirts and grubby jeans or pinstripe suits with cufflinks and tie. They see the person.

But in Parkinson's, people see the condition. It's human nature. And non-matching socks, slightly scrappy shaving, old baggy jumpers or finger marked spectacles -- pretty much my normal appearance since I work from home -- are taken as sure indicators of physical and mental disintegration. Not to me, you understand -- I couldn't give two hoots -- but to others. But it's clear that I'm not the best judge of this. What I see as vaguely artistic, perhaps slightly bohemian or simply relaxed, Claire and others see as shambolic. The tut-tutting Alice thinks I'm beyond redemption, that my lack of interest in clothes is terminal. If I was a horse, she would be plugging two rounds into a twelve bore shotgun and as we speak.

Ally an unkempt appearance to a bedraggled physiology and, before you know it, you are the subject of the chattering classes. "He's not handling it very well" or "it's the Parkinson's -- he's let himself go" seem to be common reactions. Enquiries after my health are suddenly more concerned and penetrating. I have changed from slightly untidy and eccentric academic to meths-drinking derelict. Less "Man at C&A" than "Man at DOA". Wear a jacket or a tie and suddenly it's a case of "Jon is doing really well" or "his medication is really working".

So it's off to the shops to check out the new Parkie Spring collection. New clothes for Old Shaky. Clothes that are smart, casual and above all, easy to get in and out of. Fancy buckles, ties, buttons and so forth are pointless. They make as much sense to a Parkie as a Swahili travel guide. It is a damning indictment of my disinterest that I'm shocked by the price of things. But then that's ten years of inflation for you. And since my existing wardrobe has seen the back of more than one Chancellor of the

Exchequer, I suppose I shouldn't be surprised. Everywhere I look there are bewildering clothes in every colour of the rainbow. I fleetingly look at a gilet if only to find out what it is. The sales assistant, descending with the speed of a harrier hawk has me cornered instantly.

"We do it in every size and colour" she says with the kind of plastic smile of one who will not be thwarted.

"Fine" I say "I'll take an extra large in budgie vomit"

March

Every day I think about dying. About disease, starvation, violence, terrorism, war, the end of the world. It helps keep my mind off things.

Roger McGough (b 1937)

THE WHIRRING COGS
Friday 4th March 2011

When it comes to causes for anxiety, we Parkies are spoilt for choice. Each and every day our bodies treat us to a veritable smorgasbord of personal disintegration. Where do you begin? The tremors that rule out half the items on a restaurant menu perhaps? Or how about the stiffness that clinches your hand into a fist -- perhaps the only thing I share with Mohammed Ali? No? Then there's the bradykinesia -- that feeling that you're walking through treacle -- that turns a stroll to the shops into a feat of endurance worthy of Shackleton. At least Shackleton never had to put up with the whispers and tut-tutting of people whose day has apparently been ruined by your sluggish presence in the queue at the deli counter. And that's just the obvious stuff. We have indignities aplenty to choose from. It really is Symptoms ' R ' Us. Welcome to the Bradykinesia Buffet.

For some of us, our symptoms are a source of continuing anxiety as we project into the future. Okay, I'm not crazy about any of the symptoms that seem to be available to me on a round-the-clock basis -- and very charitable of them too -- but there is one symptom above all that gives me the heebie-jeebies. I can put up with the tremors (just avoid red wine and soup), rigidity (now there's something I can make a fist of), and bradykinesia (think tortoise and hare). If I must. They're a nuisance and an embarrassment but they don't frighten me. The one that scares me most, my own personal spectre, is cognitive decline. And I don't mean forgetting where your glasses are or struggling over an obvious clue in the Times crossword. We've all done that. I mean an altogether darker place.

It may surprise readers to learn that I was once quite a bright little button. Top of the class, winner of the school English prize, occasional poet and painter before I consciously, if perversely, took 'the path less travelled' and decided to be a scientist. Even there I made a reasonable go of it, heading a research team for twelve years. So, as someone who has always had a pretty nifty roadster of a brain, any tarnishing of its gleaming powers is hard to bear. Every day I see, or think I see, new signals of impending cerebral meltdown. It's bad enough that my body seems to be fast tracking to oblivion without my brain hitching along for the ride. In my mind, Talking Heads are singing Road to Nowhere. But in reality, there is no cranial apocalypse. The truth is that this is a war of attrition. There is no intellectual Gettysburg. More a gradual retreat, the mental stragglers picked off by Parkinson's snipers.

It's a bit like watching aging sportsmen. They say that they know -- just know, intuitively -- when it's time to hang up their boots, bat, racket, or whatever. Maybe it's the same with cognitive decline. Maybe I will know when it's time to retire, or when I just can't hack it any longer. Maybe I will know when work colleagues whisper that "he just hasn't got it any more". Maybe, like Paul Collingwood with an unfamiliar run of poor scores, I will just know that the test match days are over.

Maybe it's the same with driving. Will my license be dragged kicking and screaming from my wallet by the DVLA as I rant and rage against the dying of the light? Or will it meekly capitulate, acknowledging that I just haven't got 'it' any more. And how will I know?

Or maybe I won't. Maybe rightly or wrongly I will hang on, battling against the odds, until form returns, refusing to let such hiccups finish me off. As cricketers say, form is temporary but class is permanent. Maybe I will simply refuse to acknowledge my dwindling intellect's stark advice.

Cognitive decline is my personal demon. It may be real or it may be imagined. It may be made of concrete or swirling shadows. Flesh and blood or skin and bones. But worse than the symptom itself is the fear of it. And that's very real.

CHICKEN RUN
Wednesday 9th March 2011

This is not the piece I had planned for this week but my last tract on cognitive decline seems to have put the cat amongst the pigeons. I've been surprised, humbled even, by the number of people who have e-mailed, written or phoned to check that I was okay. Clearly one should not bandy phrases like "cognitive decline" and "personal demons" around without expecting the switchboard to light up. Well, metaphorically anyway. And words like "dying", "capitulate", "rant" and "rage" are pretty much guaranteed to keep the postman busy as well. Again metaphorically. On the face of it, they don't suggest a man with all his intellectual ducks in a row.

Funnily enough, I hadn't seen it as being especially negative. But on rereading it, I will grudgingly concede that, when taken out of context, words like "meltdown", "apocalypse" and "oblivion" do rather suggest a man unravelling faster than the toilet roll in that annoying advert with the Labrador puppies. In fact this is verbiage more at home on a suicide note than a quasi-humorous weekly blog. My bad.

But to be honest, the response is typical of the Parkinson's community, or my corner of it anyway -- the sense of support from fellow Parkies, the Glasgow effect (from the World Parkinson's Congress). As I said to Biker Bob and Agnetha, it's the soldier's creed "we will not leave our wounded on the battlefield".

So don't worry -- I'm not giving up. As Winnie once said "....we shall fight on the beaches, we shall fight on the landing grounds, we shall fight in the fields and in the streets, we shall fight in the hills; we shall never surrender"

True, so true.

But there is an even more pressing problem than fighting Parkinson's. Because I wanted to talk about hens this week and I can't think of any logical link between the Battle of Britain and buying domestic fowl. Except of course that the Royal Air Force shot down so many Luftwaffe bombers that the skies of Kent resembled a chicken shoot.

Talking of chickens...

We have two. Now I have to be honest, I couldn't tell a Buff Orpington from a Scots Dumpy or a Jersey Giant from a Norfolk Grey. All I know is that we have a black hen and a brown hen. They belong to Claire. The large iridescent black hen with a bright red comb which, despite being female (you would have thought the eggs were a clue), was christened Vladimir by Catherine, our eldest. Once she went to college it was quickly renamed Blaise which, although obviously superior to Vladimir as a girl's name, was chosen for reasons that have never been adequately explained to me. Its companion is a slightly smaller tan coloured chicken called Alice. Alice also being the name of my younger daughter, this can, as you might imagine, cause some confusion. And Alex is not slow to exploit its comic potential. Shouting from the garden, in a voice loud enough to be heard in the next street that "Alice has done a poo in the flower bed" is the kind of behaviour calculated to cause the maximum level of discomfort for his elder sister. Only the fact that she has been studying the Geneva Convention in history prevents Alice from committing fratricide.

Blaise is the senior chicken, quite literally top of the pecking order. Alice does nothing without Blaise's authorisation. If Blaise takes a shine to a particular meal worm, it takes little more than a second or two of the evil eye for Alice to retreat. But for the most part they live happily enough together, bickering away like old ladies in a nursing home. In fact these are amongst the most cosseted fowl alive. They live in what I'm reliably assured is a fox-proof enclosure called an eggloo. The eggloo, its associated mesh and canopy comes to somewhere in the region of £400, an eye watering sum for a chicken coop in my view. Oh and the chickens are extra. You might have thought, for the kind of money that would have cleared the average supermarket of chickens, that the price of the Eggloo might include the occupants. Would it have hurt to throw in a couple of hens (and the odd chicken recipe for that matter)?

As I mentioned in an earlier piece, we have gone kind of organic in our house. And the chickens represent the latest staging point on that conversion. Somewhere between The Good Life and River Cottage. Since we let the chickens out in the garden regularly, they can legitimately claim to be free range. And there's no escaping the fact that free range eggs do taste better. But before the rose tinted glasses mist over completely, let's do some simple maths: two chickens -- £20 apiece. Their housing -- £400. Six months of feed -- £50. I make that £490. And what do we get in return, apart from a warm feeling inside. We have had Blaise and Alice for a little over six months. In that time, we have had approximately 200 eggs. In other words, each egg cost £2.45. A dozen would be a jawdropping £29.40. Even Karl Faberge, jeweller to the Czars, would have been hard pressed to top that. At that price we can't even afford to eat them. I'm half inclined to put them on eBay.

And I finally understand what they mean by nest egg. It would take one to buy one. A dozen eggs? I'll need your mortgage details.

BUCKET LIST
Monday 14th March 2011

I've been thinking about a bucket list recently. You know the kind of thing – all the things one wants to do before one kicks the bucket. Not that I'm planning to kick the bucket you understand. But you never know when the Almighty will tap you on the shoulder and say "game's up sonny, get your coat".

There seems to be an ongoing fashion for collecting together lists such as these, as some sort of exercise in self realisation, filled by over fertile imaginations, with activities ranging from the romantic through to the downright daft. And the Internet is full of such lists. Everything from the frankly underambitious "solving Rubik's cube" to the optimistic "walking on the moon". From a completely pointless "saying hello in fifty languages" to the at best marginally useful "learning to yodel". Some of the more ambitious want to "learn to fly an aeroplane" or maybe "break a Guinness world record". What makes librarians want to "eat fugu fish" or hairdressers "learn sword swallowing?" What do you gain? Well, apart from several pints of someone else's blood that is. But it got me thinking.

So last Saturday I sat down with a blank piece of paper and half an hour to kill between collecting Alice from the stables and taking Alex to nets. Plenty of time for a mind brimming with brilliant, expensive and, above all, creative ways of frittering away his children's inheritance. What shall we pick from the banquet of frivolity on offer?

Swimming with dolphins perhaps? Well in my case just swimming full stop would be a reasonable undertaking. Being aquatically-challenged (who are you calling a non-swimmer?), my children are well versed in their duties with respect to their father and water. Indeed, so seriously are these duties taken that Catherine and Alice are now qualified lifeguards. We have a deal -- they save my life, and I keep them in Krispy Kremes till the end of their days. This relates to any form of water. Canals, lakes, swimming pools and rivers. Wherever there is water and their father, my children are ready and waiting. No perceived emergency is too trivial. And I'm prepared to bet that we have the only bathroom in the country with a lifebelt. Yes, my swimming is that bad.

And while we're on the subject, whose idea was it to indicate the fact that you are drowning by calmly raising your arm. That's akin to signalling you are about to crash the car by switching on the air conditioning. If I'm drowning, I anticipate that my arms will more likely be engaged in unproductive panicked thrashing than calm and collected hand signals. And when it comes to attracting attention, I'm pretty confident that my shrieks and screams will have that base covered

So you'll forgive me if swimming with dolphins fails to tickle my fancy. Actually to be honest, I don't really get dolphins. In a nutshell they are large, grey and smell of fish. But you could say the same of my Great Aunt Dolly and I didn't see people at Rossington baths queueing up to swim with her.

Bungee jumping then perhaps? Always a popular choice, for those to whom the dolphins are not enough of a thrill. Again no. Precisely what thrill is derived from allowing the contents of your abdominal cavity to avalanche into your thorax? If God had meant my liver to nestle under my shoulder blades He would have put it there in the first place. And if that isn't good enough reason to avoid bungee jumping, there's always the snap crackle and pop of cerebral blood vessels subjected to this needless abuse. Oh and detached retinas. Did I mention that? When it comes to thrillseeking uses for elastic, my imagination stops at knickers and memories of bunking off PE with Maggie Braithwaite from 5C.

How about parachute jumping? Again, a few minutes of blind terror (or a few seconds if it goes wrong) attached optimistically to an oversized silk handkerchief seems to me to be on a similar level of insanity. And besides, silk only takes me back to Maggie Braithwaite.

For many people, their bucket lists are long, populated by a parade of idiotic activities. I for one do not plan to spend my declining years doing things that were too stupid to contemplate even when I was young. You have to ask yourself why so many of these activities are on the list. If they are on the list, it's because you haven't done them. And why haven't you done them? That's right -- because they were stupid ideas in the first place.

So when it comes to my bucket list, you can forget about "go to a drive-in movie" (saw Jaws in 1976, wouldn't get in the bath for weeks afterwards), "experience weightlessness" (surely that's what tequila is for), "start a blog" (been there, done that) or "find inner peace" (avoiding the local takeaway's lamb bhuna would be a good start).

No, I'll settle for Mardi Gras in New Orleans, watching the Northern lights from Scandinavia and seeing the Grand Canyon from the air. All great experiences. But there is only one experience on my list can legitimately claim to be the greatest.

Meeting The Greatest. Muhammad Ali.

TAKES ONE TO KNOW ONE
Sunday 20th March 2011

I was impressed to read that, in order to play her part in Love and Other Drugs, Anne Hathaway (and I'm sorry but I can't help thinking of Shakespeare's wife) studied Young Onset Parkinson's in some detail. She learnt the movements, the characteristic shakes and freezes. And good on her I say. These are the details that distinguish ordinary from exceptional acting. By all accounts, she captured the movements pretty well, even if she was faking it.

Of course, when you've had Parkinson's for a while, you reluctantly become adept at recognising the symptoms in others. Symptoms that barely register with the general public form part of a recognisable clinical picture to a person with Parkinson's. Within a very narrow field, you acquire the observational skills of an expert neurologist. You recognise, as though looking in a mirror, the frozen face of a fellow Parkie. You spot immediately symptoms of bradykinesia, even across a crowded room. Or the helicopter impressions our physicians call dyskinesia. And it's often not the symptoms themselves that attract your attention but the response of the individual to their symptoms. For instance, tremor may often be less obvious than the hands clenched, arms stiff posture we adopt to minimise visible signs of tremor. And tremor puts certain movements out of bounds. Those of us with a coarse tremor have learnt for instance not to put our hands in our trouser pockets in public. This creates entirely the wrong impression. And the last thing we want to do is draw attention to ourselves.

It's the same with festination, that little 'almost breaking into a run' sort of walk many of us seem to have. Straight out of the Ministry of Silly Walks. Again one can minimise it by consciously -- and -- methodically -- placing -- one -- foot -- in -- front -- of -- the -- other. But we can't keep it up for any distance. And often our balance lets us down when we walk slowly.

But what do you do when you come across a fellow sufferer? Do you greet them like a long lost brother and thereby draw attention to the symptoms they thought were invisible? Do you ignore the symptoms completely and, by your lack of response to a fellow sufferer, leave the person feeling undervalued, their suffering somehow negated? It's a difficult one. Personally, I find myself making small gestures of acknowledgement -- a squeeze of the hand or a knowing smile. Nothing more. Just something to say that I recognise them without drawing attention to either of us.

There is a man further up my street who has Parkinson's. We don't know each other but I see him slowly and laboriously carrying groceries or washing the car sometimes when I'm walking the dog. We don't speak a word but each of us nods to the other. Not an exaggerated gesture. But just ever so slightly longer and more deliberate than courtesy demands. We both know.

OVER MY DEAD BODY
Friday 25th March 2011

This probably seems a bit morbid but I have been thinking about the music I would like played at my funeral. Yes, that's what I said. Don't get me wrong - unless The Almighty has other ideas, I'd like to stick around for a good while yet. But it's still a useful exercise. Bear with me.

The problem is this. I have been to more funerals and listened to more funeral music over the last few years than I wanted to. Much more. And it strikes me that often the relatives of the deceased, their minds befuddled by the myriad arrangements and minutiae of a funeral, make snap choices of music that bear little relevance to themselves or their loved ones. Instead of memorable melodies, we get music for shopping malls.

Not for me, if you don't mind. Music means a lot to me. It has defined all the key moments in my life -- my wedding, the birth of each of my children, even the day I was diagnosed with Parkinson's. Each moment has been, in some way, marked by a piece of music. So I don't plan to enter the next world to the sound of Muzak. That's the musical equivalent of changing your Facebook status to "is dead".

But what sort of occasion would I want the funeral to be for instance?

Humorous perhaps? One last tickle of the ribs maybe. A funeral that made people laugh rather than cry? Reminiscent of the band playing Glenn Miller's "In the Mood" at Peter Sellars's funeral. Or the originally intended words on Spike Milligan's gravestone "I told you I was ill"

Perhaps they could play "Going Underground" by The Jam? Or "Another one bites the dust" by Queen? Or maybe a long guitar solo by the Grateful Dead? The possibilities are endless. Alex, my 13-year-old son, has already specified "Highway to Hell" by AC/DC for his own funeral. Believe me, that's not going to happen.

Maybe the funeral should be austere then, Gothic, bleak and sombre in the way of many northern funerals in the past. Don't forget I'm a Yorkshire boy at heart with a strong sense of place, time and the weight of generations. I know my place. The more I think about it -- and I have all those nights of Parkie insomnia to thank for this -- the more I feel drawn to gravitas, weight and majesty. Maybe black-plumed horses pulling the bier. Already I can hear my grandmother telling me not to put on airs and graces. She is right of course.

It may not be a state funeral but we still need music. And we need memorable music. Music that means something to me, for some significant reason. Can I leave it to chance? Can I be sure that my family and friends would pick appropriate tunes? Or would they have me turning in my grave before I'd even got into it?

Choosing for others is always difficult. Charged with the same task for my father-in-law some years back, we entered the church to the great theme from Elgar's first symphony, and left to Lee Marvin singing "Wandering Star". Collectively, they seemed to encapsulate the dichotomy between a World War Two boy refugee's nomadic spirit and his overwhelming desire to belong to his adopted country.

So should I just leave the choice of music to my family? Evidently, if Alex's choice is anything to go by, this is best not left in the hands of adolescent boys who listen to more heavy metal than can possibly be healthy. Alice's suggestion of "wall-to-wall Wagner" is closer to the mark but still not quite on the money. So, with that in mind, I think a pre-emptive strike is in order. Here are some of the choices I am considering. Think of it as a sort of Deceased Island Discs.

So much music has passed through my life. Pop, rock, jazz, classical and opera – you name it, I've heard it. Not to mention all those Marxist/Leninist-jazz-funk bands, Norwegian nose flute quintets, lute and bagpipe concertos and other strange hybrids. Sometimes I think that my friend Tom at the Beeb and I are the only people who listen to this stuff. A private cabinet of musical curiosities.

How do you distil all that music to a mere three meaningful snippets? So many tunes failed to make the cut. "The End" by The Doors, a wonderful song but, for reasons obvious to anyone who has listened to it, unsuitable for a funeral. Led Zeppelin's "Stairway to Heaven"? A lovely song certainly but a tad obvious? How about "Annie", that beautiful autumnal ballad by Ronnie Laine. Too short -- no time for serious blubbing. And the fact that I'm a rather chubby boy these days rules out "Hallelujah" sung by Jeff Buckley. Funerals are no place for Shrek jokes. Coldplay's "The Scientist" would be logical except for the fact that I associate it with an old friend's funeral. He was a scientist too.

So after all the deliberation, here are the results of the Parkinson's jury.

First of all, what do a film about King Arthur, a wooden opera house in Bavaria and a Melbourne brewery have in common? I'm going to have to hurry you. The answer, and my first choice of funeral music, is Siegfried's Trauermarsch from Gotterdammerung (Twilight of the Gods). Perhaps an obvious choice for a lover of Wagner but nonetheless a gorgeous, sombre, brooding theme punctuated by huge, crashing orchestra tutti. The march, first performed in Bayreuth in 1876, was chosen by John Boorman in 1981 as incidental music for Excalibur and, more recently, to advertise Carlton Draught. And why not? A tidal wave of strings and brass carrying a hero home (Siegfried not me, silly).

My second choice presents me with a dilemma. Two songs, equally beautiful but in different ways. First, and forgive me for having a Radio 2 moment is "Wild Horses" sung by Mad Hair herself Susan Boyle. This one should definitely get hankies out. Sublimely beautiful singing of what surprisingly few know is actually an old Rolling Stones number.

The other choice is another song but of a completely different type. This is Im Abendrot by Strauss -- that's Richard Strauss not waltz boy -- written towards the end of his life. Listen to Elisabeth Schwarzkopf singing it. A soprano of such luminous tone as that comes along once in a generation. I still can't decide. Oh blow it, I'll have both. After all it's my funeral.

My ...er ... fourth choice and, even if everything else changes, the only one I have definitely decided on, is Deep River, a Negro spiritual orchestrated by Sir Michael

Tippett. Sung in multipart harmony, this song has such a haunting beauty that you can't imagine any music following it.

Watch the choir of King's College Cambridge singing it on Youtube. There was nothing that would reduce my mother to tears more than the pure sound of boys singing in harmony. This would have had her in floods.

For many years, I had misheard the line "I want to cross over to the campground", that gentle metaphor for resignation to death. Every time I listened, it seemed to say "I won't go stumbling to heaven". With Parkinson's, that seems infinitely more likely.

Funeral music sorted. Job done.

MARTHA'S GIRL
Thursday 31 March 2010

Kansas 1958. In a tired wooden prairie farmhouse, Martha Boone was struggling with childbirth on a wild November night, as the wind howled outside, rattling the flaking casements. The old timber house creaked and groaned, screen door flapping, as though trying to drown out Martha's screaming and hollering.

Only married a week, she thought, and now this to show. Wed in Lawrence the past Saturday. Herself, her spouse Kyle William Boone and two bewildered anonymous witnesses dragged from Rocco's ice cream parlour over the road. In a quarter of an hour, Martha Pound was Martha Boone. No organ music, no preacher's blessing, no fine ten dollar words. No pretty dress with bows and buttons and fancy ties. And no more blazing rows with Louisa Mayberry Pound, her mother and haughty pillar of the Blood Butte Episcopalian Church. Long as her daughter was married, Louisa Mayberry could hold her head high. No more sniggering and whispering at the back of her Sunday bible class. No more rumours and poison gossip about her daughter. Her daughter was married now and respectable. And that was an end to it.

Married indeed. Even had a ring to prove it. Looked no more than a curtain ring, all worn thin, scratched and old. Her husband's great-great-grandmother Isabella had found it, all bloody brown, near Hazelton Creek in the fly-buzzing summer of 1864. She met her husband-to-be bathing in the creek the same day. Ezra Temperance Boone, though barely nineteen a weary veteran of the 33rd Virginians, had fought with Stonewall at Manassas Junction and lost two toes at Chancellorsville. How could a Southerner have such dark blue eyes, she wondered that afternoon. They courted for scarcely a month, and were married for nigh six decades, squabbling for most. Like nettles and dock she said, never saying which was which. Still she bore him seven strong sons to till the land and build the farm. Coyotes howled among the cottonwoods the night she died. In the same bed where Martha was squealing like a stuck pig.

While the wind howled outside, and Martha howled from the bedroom, Ezra's great-great-grandson paced the carpet bare outside, waiting, cigar in hand, for a baby's cry. An hour went by. And another as Martha and the storm grew more shrill. Upstairs, a window pane blew in, shattering on the floor. All the while, Injun Ida from the Iroquois reservation mopped, talked and soothed his wife through labour. Kyle William waited and fretted, walking holes in his work shoes. As the storm raged, Injun Ida poked her head round the door. Holding her hand up to stay Kyle's unasked question she spoke softly "Havin' a tough time of it – better get the doc". Ida's hands and dress were bloody.

In moments Kyle William was in the pickup, gunning the engine and crunching the failing gearbox into first. The truck spit-spluttered along Telegraph Road, dodging storm debris and weaving between rain-filled potholes.

Hammering breathlessly on Doc's door, Kyle William felt the rain and sweat running in salty rivulets down his brow. Doc tried to slow the gush of words. "Can't help quick till you speak slow" he said "now count to ten". Kyle William paused and panted. "Martha's baby's stuck, Doc" he blurted "Injun Ida says she's gonna die". Kyle William couldn't remember if Ida had said that or if he had muddled it with his fears. "Turn the truck round" said Doc "I'll get my bag of tricks"

There was only one light on in the house, alone on the prairie, picked out by the lightning. Ida met them on the porch. "She's slipping away" she said "baby won't turn". There were no sounds from the bedroom as Doc entered, followed by Ida. Kyle William stood uncertain in the doorway. "Best come in if you got any words you wanna say" said Ida. "No" said Doc "we have work to do. We'll call you when we're done" and closed the door firmly.

Kyle William cleared up the broken glass on the landing, busying himself with small tasks and listening, half hopeful half desperate, with one ear for Martha's wailing. Hoping for reassurance. Some sign that God was merciful. He promised to be a good husband, a better son, to go to church even. Anything that would keep Martha from dying. As the night wore on, he promised everything he had and didn't have as the silence from the bedroom deepened, draining his hopes away.

He woke with a start. Somehow in the long night of pleas, promises and bargains, he had fallen asleep curled up on the landing. The night was over and the still grey daylight had woken Ma Lawrence's rooster. The storm had passed. One of the cottonwoods had fallen. For a moment, Kyle William thought of the animals in the barn. The thoughts of a single man still, after a week, unfamiliar with marriage. Looking out of the window, he saw his pickup and the events of the night came tumbling back like autumn leaves.

Doc was seated motionless on Isabella's prayer stool outside the bedroom, bloodied sleeves rolled up and head in his hands. The bedroom door was firmly closed and the room was silent. As Kyle William tiptoed toward him, Doc stirred and rubbed his stubbled chin. Neither met the other's gaze. "Doc?" said Kyle William. There was a long pause. "Kyle William" said Doc, lighting a cigarette and holding out the silver case. Kyle William shook his head. "It's morning, Doc" he said. Doc rubbed his eyes "Been a long night" he said "you were sleeping". Kyle William stood, aware of his heartbeat, afraid to ask the question, as though Martha was still alive as long as he did not speak. He opened his mouth but no words came. "Go in" said Doc, expressionless, gesturing with his cigarette toward the door.

Injun Ida opened the door. She pointed to the bed, then turned to open the shutters. Martha was still, all colour drained, her arms by her side. Strange, thought Kyle William, that death should be so calm. No terrors pursued her into the next world. The face of sleep. Kyle William knelt beside the bed, his shoulders heaving as he fought back the tears.

Injun Ida turned. "Why the tears?" Kyle William looked up. "She's sleeping. Hard time, but she'll make it". As she said so, Martha stirred. Eyes half open, she smiled slowly. The prettiest smile Kyle William had ever seen. He grasped her hand and sobbed. "That's no good" whispered Martha "your daughter doesn't want to see tears". From a crib by the window, Ida lifted a tiny bundle. "Kyle William Boone" said Martha "meet Annabel Mayberry Boone".

As he held his daughter to his chest, the sun broke through the clouds and the baby opened her eyes. "Annabel Mayberry Boone" he repeated. And for that brief moment, Martha, Kyle and Annabel were the only people in the world.

"But that's her baptism name before God" said Martha "not for us".

"For us, she'll be Annie Mae" said Martha.

"Angel Annie" whispered Kyle William Boone "Angel Annie".

April

The life of every man is a diary in which he means to write one story, and writes another; and his humblest hour is when he compares the volume as it is with what he vowed to make it.

James M. Barrie (1860 - 1937)

PHONE TROUBLE
Thursday 5th April 2011

On the whole, I like gadgets. Breadmakers, espresso machines, iPads, DVD players and so on. But I'm having a real problem with my phone. It's not giving too much away to say that it's a well-known type of fruit. No, not mango, wiseguy.

It has a touch screen, and that's pretty much where the trouble starts. Actually the trouble starts a little earlier because, like most phones these days, the mere act of facilitating long-distance verbal communication is the least significant dimension of its functionality. If a phone was just a phone, it would all be easy. Press some numbers and, hey presto, you can talk to your friend. Press another button to stop talking. Easy. Even Alexander Graham Bell would have got it.

On the other hand, Bell would have been at sea in his local Carphone Warehouse. He wouldn't know where to start. I don't even think you can buy a phone that just makes phone calls any more. Indeed the mere mention of such an idea in a mobile phone shop is, like a Bateman cartoon, enough to bring the storeroom staff out to gawp. Even the humblest phones seem to have more functions than anyone could possibly need. Faced with this mind-boggling array of largely superfluous functionality, it's easy to get lost. Like my mother-in-law who, coming relatively late to the technological age, bought herself a a wireless printer. It worked fine as a printer but, no matter how many buttons she pressed, it still wouldn't tune into Gardeners Question Time.

My phone -- and I only call it a phone for want of a better word -- can record music, play music and, for all I know, compose music. It can play backgammon, chess, and checkers. When it comes to cards, I have the full resources of a moderately sized casino at my fingertips. Or I can race a Formula One car. I can Google, Yahoo, Bing or Ask. I can twitter like a song thrush, should the urge take me. I can take photos, make videos, edit and share. I can write letters to my MP, file his terse replies, calculate compound interest on my mortgage shortfall, and prepare slides for my lecture to the psychology students. Deep in its little memory banks are every person I have ever phoned or who has phoned me. Never mind their phone number, this will tell me their horoscope, their weakness for Belgian chocolates and the fact that they have an irrational phobia about cotton wool. It will even show me a picture of where they live. Short of making coffee, there seems to be next to nothing this phone can do. It took less processing power than this to put Neil Armstrong on the moon. The smug little blighter even calls itself a smart phone.

I don't even need to touch the phone. Like Nipper, it responds to its master's voice. Well, sort of. If I ask it to "call Imogen", it invariably asks me if I mean "I-Mow-Gun". Firstly, I don't know anybody of that name and, secondly, if I had meant I-Mow-Gun I would have said I-Mow-Gun. "No" I shout back. Undeterred, it asks me if perhaps I mean "Indian". It misinterprets my unnecessarily exasperated "no, I blooming well do not" as "yes" and, before I have worked out precisely why it would ask such a question in the first place, I find myself apologising to Suresh at the Taj Mahal Tandoori for the eye watering barrage of profanities I have inadvertently subjected him to. And the thing calls itself a smart phone? I'll be the judge of that I think.

And, if I didn't know better, I'd say the phone was stalking me. It's as though it has some sixth sense, it knows exactly where I am to within a metre of two. My father was mightily impressed until I told them that this was the same technology used to guide cruise missiles. "Better switch it off then" he said, nervously looking out of the window, half expecting the sky to darken with incoming Tomahawks. He shouldn't worry -- they're probably heading to the Indian takeaway anyway.

Parkies and touchscreen technology do not go well together. One misplaced tremor and events quickly snowball out of control. One brief shudder in the middle of a game of solitaire and I find I have just bought 2000 shares in Armenian zinc. I can be entering a new contact into my address book one minute. A second later and I find I have erased all my friends from F to J. Written out of my life faster than a politburo reshuffle.

Anything involving numbers is dangerous. Telephoning is one thing -- a swift apology for a wrong number and no harm done. Double digits elsewhere can mean deep water. Especially if you hit return instead of backspace. You try turning away 11 family size pepperoni pizzas at the door.

Being at least nominally a phone you might imagine that being able to make telephone calls was a given. Any phone worthy of the name should be able to make a fist of that. Not so. Outside the house, reception is adequate. Well, adequate if you are standing so close to a base station that you can almost hear the crackle of your own synapses. Clearly little of the innovative technology on offer to the manufacturers has gone into those components of the phone that actually make phonecalls. Consequently there are only a handful of hotspots in our house where this modest telephonic feat can be comfortably achieved -- in the living room (standing next to the fireplace), in the conservatory (just south of the tall bookcase), in the loft (next to the water tank) and in the downstairs toilet. But only when seated. With both arms raised. On Tuesdays.

TRAINSPOTTING
Sunday 10th April 2010

A couple of weekends back, we took a train to Bath, my alma mater. The journey, on one of the fastest lines, essentially Brunel's old Great Western Railway, could have taken a little over an hour. But this weekend we chose to take a step back in time as well. We were to travel to and from Bath by steam.

As I have said before, the railways are in my blood. My grandfather, great grandfather and great great-grandfather all built locomotives at the plant works in Doncaster. As a child, I was lucky enough to catch the tail end of the steam era, watching the expresses thunder past at night, catching the whiff of steam and burning coal as they did.

So when our friends Eve and Drew booked the trip as a treat, I have to confess that I was more excited than I let on. The locomotive pulling the train was 34067 Tangmere and, indulge me for a moment, if I tell you it was a 128 ton, air-smoothed Battle of Britain class 4-6-2 Bulleid Light Pacific, a with a water capacity of 4500 gallons and a coal capacity of 5 tons generating a boiler pressure of 280 psi and tractive effort of 31,050 lb from three 16 x 24 inch cylinders.

For many of you, that last sentence is meaningless gibberish. I might as well be speaking in tongues. But for those in the know, it reads like a Shakespeare sonnet. Tangmere, named after the Sussex airfield, was built in September 1947 at Brighton, and operated mainly from the Stewarts Lane Depot in Battersea, until the end of 1962 when it was transferred to the Salisbury Depot on the West Of England lines until November 1963, when it was withdrawn from service and taken to Eastleigh for scrapping. Somehow it eluded destruction until restoration began in 1980.

There was a heavy frost when we arrived, shivering, at Three Bridges for the 7.52 departure for Bath. Needless to say, and presumably in an effort to preserve absolute authenticity of the steam age experience, the train was late, finally leaving at 8.30 due to brake problems at Purley. The station was a remarkable sight for a Saturday morning. In addition to the usual bewildered foreign tourists "Ees zees ze Gatvick Express?", there were a huge number of trainspotters.

I have to be careful what I say here because one of our good friends Trev the Train is of that persuasion and I know Trev dips into my writings. But even Trev would acknowledge that trainspotters are a breed apart. And although many do not wear the eponymous garment, there was nonetheless a strong whiff of anorak that morn. And each had a camera. Not just any camera mind you -- none of your happy snappies here. No, these were cameras worthy of a Princess Diana photo opportunity or a Naomi Campbell court appearance. And everywhere along the track to Bath, on every bridge and at every station, in fields, cuttings and buildings were men (and they nearly always are men) with tripods supporting cameras the size of mediaeval siege artillery.

There is also a high proportion of beards, I've noticed.

As it was a treat, we travelled first class, waving regally to the trainspotters as we passed. Danish pastries and coffee on tables covered with white linen, although smuts from the engine soon put paid to that and reminded me why the end of the steam era was not universally mourned. Even as scheduled at 4½ hours it was, to say the least, a leisurely journey. Languid even. With water stops at Preston Park, Botley, and Salisbury punctuating the journey, we passed gently through Worthing, Chichester, Romsey, Bathampton and on to Bath in time for a late lunch.

But this was not a journey for people in a hurry. We listened to the rustle of newspapers and the chuff chuff of the engine as it climbed past Hassocks to the Clayton Tunnel, working hard against the gradient, then whistling in locomotive glee as we topped the hill and coasted past Fishergate Halt and on to Shoreham. Even the conversation was from another time. We talked wistfully of the Ealing comedies, classic cars, canal boats and, perhaps distastefully, of great train crashes. Nobody used the D word. That's diesel for the non-anoraks among you. Although there was a buffet car, not many made use of it. Most had bought their sandwiches, neatly wrapped in tinfoil in snap closed Tupperware containers.

Our carriage was the only one in which the heating worked. Having said that, there was no way of controlling the heating. It was 'On' or 'Off'. Off meant teeth chattering for five hours. On meant skin grafts -- visions of World War II fighter pilots and early plastic surgery.

It was much colder on the return journey. A clear sky and a beautiful full moon rising over Salisbury had everyone reaching for the cameras again. As with the outward journey, cameras followed the train's every move. As we pulled into each station, a storm of flashbulbs greeted us.

Dark by now, there was an arctic draught for most of the journey. It didn't matter how many windows we closed. It was only when we made an unscheduled stop at Angmering that anyone noticed that the outer carriage door was wide open, flapping in the wind. I presume we hadn't lost any passengers overboard although nobody seemed in a hurry to do a headcount. Still, if we had lost any passengers, I'm sure it would have been captured on camera.

Our carriage, like so many, was built in Doncaster. For three quarters of a century, my ancestors worked there building locomotives, trains and carriages. My great-grandfather Tom was a 'waggon builder' (sic) working in the Lower Turnery for some forty years. Chances are he built this carriage. Maybe, during a break sixty years ago, he even sat at the same seat, in his overalls supping his tea for a minute.

One can but dream and steam engines are the stuff of dreams.

MRS O'HARA'S TURKEY
Friday 15th April 2011

There is something about Parkinson's that makes you nostalgic for the past. Perhaps it's a desire for healthier times? Maybe it is just a reflection of increasing age. I was in Bristol last week, filming a video about GDNF and Parkinson's. Picking up a friend along the way, we drove through Marlborough where, for five years, I went to school. As my mind wandered, as it so often does, I found myself thinking about chemistry and cookery.

My old chemistry teacher felt that cooking was nothing more than applied biochemistry and that a kitchen was merely a specialised laboratory. Take the right ingredients, follow the recipe exactly and the results would be predictable and reproducible. He took pleasure in showing us home-made mayonnaise whilst explaining the difference between suspensions and emulsions. It was the same jar he had shown to the previous year. And the year before that.

Of course there were no sell-by-dates in those days. And precious little in the way of Health and Safety regulations, their absence attested to by the pools of mercury beneath the floorboards in 11 F. Not that anyone would have even considered for a second actually tasting the mayonnaise. Especially since his vinaigrette, made using glacial acetic acid (don't try this at home. No, really, don't try this at home) ate holes in the kitchen linoleum.

Still, Dr Richards kept you on your toes. Double chemistry on a Thursday afternoon was, mayonnaise or no mayonnaise, a signal that the weekend began there. His classes felt like a party. He would have us all breathing helium and squeakily pretending to be cartoon characters. Or he would 'accidentally' spill ether, letting it flow along the bench to the Bunsen. He balked at nothing. We would make ammonium dichromate volcanoes, watching the orange crystals become mountains of green ash. Or he would flick lumps of sodium the size of sugar cubes into the swimming pool and take cover as columns of water worthy of a depth charge erupted near the diving board. He even taught us how to make gunpowder. For him the chemistry was everything. For us as pupils, it was all smells and bangs. But the fact that I remember this forty years later suggests that something must have stuck.

Which is more than can be said Dr Richards's cooking. Although a consummate showman in the lab, his cooking disappointed. When the chemistry club met at his house on Saturday evenings, there were no culinary pyrotechnics. His cooking was a demonstration of chemistry in control. And we all wanted chemistry very much out of control. We wanted danger in the kitchen. Most people, not surprisingly, don't. Mrs Lowndes certainly didn't.

Did I ever tell you about Mrs Lowndes? No? Okay, bear with me.

When I was at school, we had three options on a Wednesday afternoon: Cadet Force, Social Services or Works Group. The Cadet Force included Signals (messing around with radios mainly), Royal Engineers (mostly learning how to hotwire cars) or regular army (marching up and down the parade ground and shouting a lot -- mainly for terminally unimaginative bullies). The Works Group and Social Services were a sort of alternative to cadets for conscientious objectors and those with higher aspirations in life than marching and shouting. Over the course of my time at school, I spent time in each of the three options.

Works Group was essentially a means of getting all the odd jobs around the school done -- painting white lines around parking spaces, raking gravel, unblocking drains and washing the headmaster's Daimler.

Social Services entailed visiting old people in the town, helping dig their garden and generally making oneself useful. In return, you got a cup of tea and a slab of cake. That was pretty much the deal. Some of the socially serviced would supervise closely, peering suspiciously from behind the nets for signs of slacking among the namby-pamby college boys.

It was during my time doing social services that I met Mrs Lowndes. Unlike some of the old ladies, who inflicted working conditions modelled on the Bridge on the River Kwai, she was the kind of lady I would have happily adopted as an additional grandmother. She had a good sized garden but, apart from a few token minutes of leaf raking or tentative trowel work in the herbaceous borders, expected nothing more than a chance to chat. We talked about everything and anything. She plied me with Victoria sponge while she told wonderful stories, but none better than that of her friend Mrs O'Hara.

Siobhan O'Hara, although Irish, had lived in Britain most of her life, since leaving County Kerry in 1905. Her husband Dermot, too fond of his whiskey, had died in February 1945 and her daughters had left home. Christmas 1945 promised to be frugal and lonely. No Dermot and no whiskey even -- import duty was so outrageous that it was impossible to import. Rationing was still in place and there were coupons for everything.

So imagine her surprise when, a few days before Christmas, a man knocked on her door to deliver an enormous turkey. "Sent by friends across the water" he said. There was a note with it, addressed to Dermot -- "Happy Christmas from Sean and Colleen. Make sure it's well stuffed". Mrs O'Hara had somehow forgotten to tell Sean of his friend Dermot's death. But the gift of a turkey, especially one so large, in such times of need, was not something to be spurned. She tipped the man, took the turkey to the kitchen and wrote a hasty note to Sean and Colleen.

Siobhan invited her neighbours to join her for Christmas, to share this unexpected bounty. She rubbed the bird in butter, lit the gas in the oven and set the turkey cooking. Under the stairs she found an old unopened bottle of cream sherry and poured herself a glass. The neighbours arrived, the sherry was passed round and conversation flowed well enough that she could take briefly to the kitchen to check progress.

Just as she stood up, an explosion tore through the back of the house. The doors rattled, the house shook and windowpanes cracked. There were screams and panic, quickly subsiding when no one was hurt. The kitchen was devastated. All the windows were shattered, the oven was ablaze and the kitchen table, set and decorated with crackers, was on its side. The turkey was nowhere to be seen and the oven door was in the garden.

The fire brigade scratched their chins, mystified by the chain of events. A gas explosion of some sort was their considered conclusion. Mrs O'Hara went to her neighbours while the fire brigade cleared up. She made the best of Christmas, bewildered by the chain of events

On Boxing Day, the phone rang. It was Sean offering his condolences over Dermot's death and passing on seasons greetings. "Did you enjoy the turkey?" he asked. Mrs O'Hara explained what had happened. "Did you not get the message about making sure it was well stuffed?" asked Sean. Mrs O'Hara had to admit that she had not paid attention to it.

"Oh" said Sean and paused "then you wouldn't have found the bottle of whiskey inside"

THE NIGHT VISITORS
Unpublished – April 2011

Along that hazy edge of waking dreams
They slowly shuffle, snuffle by my head
Matt tangled hair, soft whispers, blinking eyes
Soft playful warm breath on my ears and neck
Each night they come by unmade firm appointment
The night visitors, the wild things' soft procession.

Sleep. Don't get me started. Or rather do. Because insomnia is the bane of Parkinson's. Whether due to the condition itself or to overexuberant medication, many of us find it difficult to go to sleep, difficult to stay asleep, and difficult to get at back to sleep. I'm typing this at 5 AM. I have been awake listening to the nightly creaks and groans of the house since 3 AM. The click of the central heating thermostat, the drip of a tap, the low hum of the fridge. The soundtrack of the night, senses sharpened by the darkness. Now I'm listening to the first stirrings of the dawn chorus.

There is a cruel irony in this because, as difficult as it is to sleep at night, the opposite holds true during the day. Many of us find ourselves dozing off at times both appropriate and inappropriate. To fall asleep watching Emmerdale is entirely understandable, so soporific is the pace. You don't need Parkinson's to do that. But to be overwhelmed by sleep during live coverage of the Japanese tsunami is somnolence of a different order. And all due to a broken night's sleep. Did I say broken? What I meant was shattered into a thousand tiny crystal shards.

If it were only the sleep loss, that would be bad enough. But for some like my friend Jack, in that ill-defined place between sleep and wake, the mind plays tricks. The folds in the curtains and bedclothes take on shapes. The computer's blue lights become eyes and the shadows assume forms. In that twilight of his imaginings, strange forest creatures surround him. Imagine the creatures in Maurice Sendak's Where the Wild Things Are or the Gruffalo, or more accurately several Gruffaloes, crowded around the foot of his bed. Sometimes he almost laughs. Asleep or awake, it's immaterial. Whether of his dreams or of his waking, they are his nightly companions.

Jack's night visitors are benign, friendly almost. They mean no harm and merely nuzzle him with playful interest. He has learnt to live with their nightly snuffling. If his imagination has brought them into being it can send them to bed too. But he is lucky. For others, the night visitors can be terrifying figures, dementors and wraiths invading that twilit space between sleep and wake. But whether dreams, hallucinations or nightmares, the vocabulary is unimportant. They are still uninvited guests in his consciousness.

What brings these creatures out? What draws them from the deepest recesses of our subconscious to the realm of the tangible, the tactile even? What perverted neurochemistry conjures these realities from our psyche? Once again, the finger points at dopamine. Not in the basal ganglia, where its welcome presence prevents us from freezing, speeds our walking and stops our shakes. But in the mesolimbic pathway where, in puckish fashion, it brings chaos to order. The mesolimbic pathway, projecting from the midbrain to the limbic system, fuels our imagination, feeds urges and pumps up our creativity. When we experience pleasure, it comes from here. This is the reward system in the brain. Too little dopamine and we are dull creatures of apathy. We need the limbic system like a drug. And a drug it is, for this is the site in the brain where drugs of abuse act. When we feel a high, it is here. And this is a site where our own drugs, the very medications that keep us moving, can also act.

Nothing is free. We need our drugs to keep us moving. Their actions in the basal ganglia keep one foot moving in front of the other. But their actions in the mesolimbic system can change us too, in subtle ways -- making us people we would rather not be and taking us to places we would rather not go. Too much dopamine here and our imagination runs riot, our creativity knows no bounds, and our urges are unchecked. This is the path of obsession, of vivid dreams and hallucinations. This is the playground of Titania and Oberon, of Mustardseed and Moth. The home of the night visitors, playing in the forests of the mind.

So can we move easily without this tiresome mental baggage?

Yes. It's all a question of balance, carefully titrating what we need to keep our bodies moving and our minds still rather than the opposite. It is estimated by some that vivid dreams and hallucinations are amongst the most underreported side-effects of medication. Is it a fear of madness, of stigma or a dread of consequences that prevents us from telling a physician? Maybe all of these things. Perhaps we really believe we are alone.

We are not. You are not.

And be absolutely clear on this -- this is not the path to madness. Merely the price we pay for movement. A high price certainly, but nothing more. Recognise it for what it is.

Do not be afraid. It's just dopamine, our old friend. And we should know his tricks by now.

As Puck concludes, in Shakespeare's Midsummer Night's Dream:

If we shadows have offended,
Think but this, and all is mended,
That you have but slumber'd here
While these visions did appear.
And this weak and idle theme,
No more yielding but a dream

GERIATRIC DUGONG NECKLACE FIASCO
Thursday 21st April 2011

When my children were younger we would play a word game in the car to make the journey pass more quickly. I Spy never really cut the mustard with my lot so we invented a game of acronyms. We would take the three letters at the end of each number plate we saw e.g. ABC from the plate A123 ABC. The game was to try and produce scientifically plausible nonsense from the acronym. The kind of stuff popular in adverts for Flabfighter diets or improbably shaped exercise equipment, grinningly demonstrated by Barbie and Ken lookalikes with pearl white teeth. So ABC might stand for Activated Blubber Cancelling or Arsenic-Based Corpuscles or Advanced Buttock Crinkles. There were no rules. The winner was the person who defined their most outrageous advertising based acronym or got the biggest laugh. Nobody kept score. Of course the fact that we were using numberplates limited us to TLAs (Three Letter Acronyms, or Turbot-Laced Abdominals as the junior advertising executives swiftly proffer from the back seat).

An acronym that has been much on my mind recently is GDNF. Despite the wealth of offerings from my offspring (Goat Dung Neutralising Fishscales or Geriatric Dugong Necklace Fiasco), GDNF actually stands for Glial Derived Neurotrophic Factor. And, for those of you not in the loop so to speak, the buzz on GDNF is interesting to say the least.

Let's start from basics: All existing Parkinson's treatments either treat symptoms, and goodness knows there are enough to choose from. Or they claim on often scanty evidence to be disease modifying. "Disease modifying" are really just fancy words for "might slow down the rate of progression of Parkinson's". The jury is pretty much out on disease modifying drugs. Sure, there are some but the word is bandied about too much for my liking. Either way, current drugs either mask existing symptoms or slow the appearance of new symptoms. And that's it.

GDNF looks, on the face of it, to be an altogether different beastie. Along with a number of other neurotrophic factors GDNF has to be shown in the lab to make nerves regenerate or grow back. Most of the lab-based work has concentrated on spinal injuries, trying to bridge the neuronal gap in severed spinal cords. But it seems that other nerve cells can be made to grow back as well. Such as dopamine cells. The claims for GDNF go some way beyond "symptom treatment" or even "disease modification". These guys are raising the bar and words like "disease reversal", "miracle" and even, whisper it quietly, "cure". Yes you read that right, the word cure is being used. Excited? Thought you might be.

I'd better give you some more background. About a decade ago, Stephen Gill at Frenchay Hospital near Bristol conducted a clinical trial on a handful of patients. I won't bore you with the gory details, but the gist of it was that he injected GDNF into the brains of around half a dozen patients. And they got significantly better.

But that was nearly 10 years ago, I hear you say. Why the buzz now? Well, for several years after the initial trial, GDNF was unavailable for human use. In essence the pause button was pressed on all further research. But that no longer holds. GDNF can now be tested in man again and Stephen Gill is looking to fund a bigger trial.

Now I'm not one for wanton hyperbole as you know. I don't know whether this is the beginning of the end for Parkinson's or not, so I'm just going to let you form your own judgements. Take a look at the before-and-after videos on Youtube and tell me that you're not impressed.

I was very impressed. So much so that I went down to Frenchay a couple of weeks back to meet Stephen Gill and to film a video appeal for funds to ensure that this research can go ahead. I'll let you know when the video is available and then you can feast your eyes on Tom, Jo and yours truly (looking particularly dapper in a jacket and tie, though I say so myself) as we tell you what we think about GDNF and why this study needs support. Okay, I know surgery isn't for everyone. And I'm sure many of us feel that we need neurosurgery like a hole in the head -- sorry, couldn't resist. But even the most squeamish of us would surely concede that we need to do the trials.

These trials don't come cheap as you can imagine and funding is being sought from a range of sources. More importantly, these trials have the backing of the CPT (that's Cure Parkinson's Trust by the way, not Cuboidal Parsnip Telemetry, the latest offering from the back seat). But a great deal more money is needed. Please pledge your support.

Maybe when your head is in a hole you do need a hole in the head...

THE WEE WEE HOURS
Tuesday 26th April 2011

When I was younger, much younger, I would sleep till the crack of noon. My mother, wont to snoozing after teatime, would wake me around three in the afternoon, on the grounds that we would otherwise not find a time window during the day when we were both awake. Being my mother, she felt that it was not unreasonable that there should be at least some narrow window in the day for parent-child interaction. That was forty years ago. Now, since my mother went for the big sleep, to paraphrase Chandler, I have been unable to sleep. She would have appreciated the irony.

Now I wake around five. In the morning that is. The birds are not yet bored of singing and the dawn chorus is mutinous. I glance over at the alarm clock. A brief misreading of the time has me bolt upright as though slapped across the face by a wet halibut. And, having once been genuinely wakened at university by an unprovoked early-morning halibut assault, I'm well placed to draw the simile. It doesn't matter that it's the weekend, I am now wide-awake. Sleep is no longer an option.

Usually I'm the only one awake. Time was, when Alex was a toddler, that mornings were very different. Always a rather obsessional toddler, his morning rituals, in particular, were immutable: When he woke, too often early, he insisted on a drink of milk. He would rouse me and we trooped downstairs in tandem, him first. I would deposit him on one corner of the kitchen counter and fetch a beaker from the cupboard. This had to be submitted for his inspection. If it passed muster, I would give him the anti-spill lid and fill the cup with milk. The milk was then to be warmed for exactly thirty seconds in the microwave and presented to him for attachment of the lid. If all was satisfactory, I was permitted – at his discretion - to make coffee for myself. As with the milk, the process was conducted under almost rabbinical supervision. We then returned upstairs with the drinks, taking care to avoid the bottom step (apparently, blue monsters slept beneath and were easily roused). Alex would then fetch Claire's neck support pillow and wrestle his sleepy mother up to the vertical. I carefully positioned his cup on the adjacent table on a green mat, with the handle toward him. He would then make himself comfortable on Claire's lap and taste his milk. If all was well, he would signify that we might now drink our coffee. A failure of any part of this process or, worse still, any change in the order would provoke a tantrum of nuclear proportions. I was reprimanded on one occasion for not being aware that the monsters had moved and were now in residence beneath the second step. And they were now green. This tended to make mornings rather gruelling. But strangely I rather miss them.

Sometimes I will make coffee, while at other times I just write. Occasionally I will traipse down to the kitchen and feed the dog. Flora, a poodle intellectual, and named after the demon daughter in The Turn of the Screw, watches and dribbles like one of Pavlov's canines until I signal that she may tuck in. The smell of coffee makes me dribble too as often as not. Dog fed, I check on the chickens. Two eggs this morning, fresh and warm. I write the date on each and place them in the crock before heading upstairs for the everyday morning treasure hunt. Most mornings my glasses are the quarry, typically being found (a) on my head, (b) by the TV remote or even, as on one disquieting occasion (c) in the fridge next to yesterday's lasagne. Today I am searching for two rotigotine patches I had shakily readied for use after my shower. They are nowhere to be seen. I even check the dog, who has been known to eat them, mistaking them for sweet wrappers.

I return to my laptop just as the alarm comes on. John Humphreys is subjecting some back-bench unfortunate to the kind of grilling I am about to give the bacon. Five minutes later and both are crispy. And Alice is in the bathroom. It doesn't matter when those five minutes are taken. I can guarantee with absolute certainty that Alice will be in the shower, having miraculously, and stealthily, gone from a slumber bordering on coma to truculent occupation of the bathroom in a matter of minutes. Any brief thoughts of ablutions that I might have entertained are dashed on the rocks of experience. For Alice is not one to whom the five-minute shower has any meaning. Popes have been elected in less time than it takes Alice to shower. This is less a matter of simple cleanliness than an opportunity to see just how many balms, salves, unguents, potions, astringents and emollients can be applied to one face. When I suggest that she might like to apply the same diligence to her chemistry revision, I am treated to the kind of look that would curdle milk.

Only when I pull on my underpants does the rustle alert me to the location of my mislaid patches – one on each cheek, like punctuation. This is not a prescribed location and the skin is raw where I tear off the patches. I ask Alice for some soothing balm, without being overly detailed as to the location of the skin in question. Bewildered by this unexpected parental interest in cosmetics, she suggests one with guava and avocado extracts. Alice is at pains to tell me this will also make my skin glow and look radiant. Since the skin is already throbbing, I am in no hurry to have it glow like a Japanese nuclear power station. And the world is not ready for the sight of my bottom, radiant or not.

The discussion wakes Claire. She sniffs. "What's that smell?" she asks. "Guava and avocado" I reply.

"Oh, you needn't have" she says "I was just going to have toast".

May

If I'm honest, this has been bugging me for a while. When you have a chronic illness like Parkinson's, it inevitably conditions the way people think about you. For some, it makes little difference. They see me not the condition. Others, who know me less well, cannot see beyond the shakes and blank expression. I don't blame them -- it's understandable. But what really bugs me is people saying "you're very brave" or words to that effect. They mean no harm but it's not a badge I accept.

Bravery, to me, is something quite different. Bravery is about choice, not force of circumstances. I did not choose to have Parkinson's. It was not a brave decision. It's just something that I have to put up with.

No, this is not bravery. Bravery is my grandfather, volunteering for the Kings Own regiment in 1914. Bravery is being gassed at Loos in 1915. Bravery is spending months in a military hospital coughing his lungs up but still believing the price of courage was not too high. That was bravery.

ANNE OSMIAH
Monday 2nd May 2011

Anne Osmiah may sound like an Arab intellectual. Somebody you would quite like to meet perhaps. But the truth is quite different. My acquaintance with Anne Osmiah has been gradual. I can't even remember the point at which her insidious influence became manifest. But for many Parkies, she will become part of our lives, gradually stealing one of our five senses -- a fifth of our connection with the outside world. At first, you won't even recognise her.

Anne Osmiah, which is what my voice recognition software chooses to call anosmia, is often one of the earliest symptoms of Parkinson's. The word anosmia is derived from the Greek and means, in plain language, 'absence or loss of sense of smell'.

Anyone unlucky enough to be familiar with my socks and shoes might reasonably construe that anosmia was a blessing rather than a handicap. Imagine a combination of ripe Gorgonzola and one of those strange lilies at Kew Gardens that flowers once a century and smells like a zombie. That would be my feet. When Richard Reid tried to detonate explosives in his shoes on a flight, my wife Claire commented that I wouldn't even need the explosives. The mere act of removing my cricket trainers would be enough to bring down most airliners.

As my sense of smell has gradually taken its leave, I have found myself inadvertently upping the anti, so to speak. Flowers have lost their scent. Perfumes no longer hold any allure. Where once I would add a mere dab of aftershave to my face, now I apply cologne as though basting a chicken. We have to drive with the windows open.

But worst of all, I have lost my ability to smell cheeses. A small price to pay you might think, but to me there is no finer way of ending a meal than with a plate of cheeses and a decent claret, port or dessert wine.

But it was not always thus. I came to cheese relatively late in life. Well, smelly cheese certainly. Growing up in Doncaster in the 1960s, there was no cheese to speak of. Or perhaps my parents, of Yorkshire and Lancashire stock, didn't hold truck with fancy foreign foodstuffs. My overwhelming memory was of cheddar (and I write that with a small C because I don't think it had been anywhere near the gorge itself) and Cheshire. I loved Cheshire and would take small pieces to my bedroom to eat, hoping my mother would not notice the tell-tale crumbs from the refrigerator. The cheddar rarely had a higher calling than cheese on toast, or Welsh rarebit as my mother would call it, lending it an entirely undeserved sophistication. On high days and holy days there would be Stilton. But as with our holidays, the Stamford family cheese board remained rooted within these sceptered isles. Occasionally, in what she saw as a nod towards European style, my mother would buy smoked Austrian cheese or Edam from Hodgson and Hepworth on Frenchgate. But this was a comparative oasis within the greater Doncaster Metropolitan area. Venture out to Cantley, Woodlands or Balby and you were in a cheese wasteland.

Very occasionally my mother would bring back something truly new. I remember the first time I saw a Camembert in our kitchen, my father viewing it like an unexploded land mine. We were going on holiday to France in a few weeks time and my mother thought it best to prime our palates. Even for someone as persuasive as my mother, there was a limit to how many things could credibly be dismissed with "it tastes like chicken".

But if the Camembert offended my father's sensitive nasal apparatus -- and this is a man who would make my mother cook sprouts in the garden -- the onslaught that followed in France itself was like an olfactory Passchendaele. Camembert and Brie were for wimps, French cheese for foreigners. The market stalls in Dinard groaned under the weight of Fourme D'Ambert, Pont L'Eveque and Reblochon. Cheeses in every shape and consistency imaginable. Some oozing from ashen crusts or furry with unfamiliar moulds. Squares, circles and ovals made from the milk of more or less any animal that lactates. Cheeses with a pungency that brings tears to eyes and fades loose furniture covers. The kind of cheeses that should be subject to rulings from the Geneva Convention. Angry, testy little cheeses that threatened to stick in your throat. My father, still unconvinced by Camembert, viewed a Pont L'Eveque as a bridge too far. He stared in horror as my brother poked at a particularly vivid example. "Don't do that Charlie" he said "you'll only annoy it". I think he half expected it to follow us back to the cottage.

Last weekend, for old times' sake, I treated myself to a modest piece of Stinking Bishop. And although I could barely smell it, I was evidently in a subset of one. Claire's reaction was that "something has died in the fridge" while Alice asked if the dog had soiled the carpet.

Joking aside, anosmia is a problem for Parkies. You only notice the sense of smell by its absence -- when you can't smell the flowers, bread baking, vanilla pods, or roast beef. Rats deprived of their sense of smell become depressed. So can humans. It is estimated that anosmia is one of the earlier symptoms of Parkinson's and that one in three people with Parkinson's has anosmia. It could be higher. I would be interested to know.

So if you see me in the street, come up and say hello. I'll be easy to recognise -- I'll be the one that smells like a cricket trainer full of cheese and doused in Armani. Try to stand upwind.

PRAETEXTATUS
Wednesday 11th May 2011

It's been an interesting sort of week one way or another. After weeks of classes with the catechists, Alex had his confirmation service on Sunday. Straightforward enough you might think but, as usual, events and circumstances conspired to make this more challenging/entertaining than it needed to be.

The last class was on Tuesday and, barring accidents, everything was set for Sunday. Along with eight other confirmation candidates, their families and friends, everything was converging on St Dunstan's.

Confirmation in the Catholic Church involves the selection of a saint's name for yourself, the idea being that you pick someone appropriate to your aspirations. Catherine, our elder daughter and a keen musician chose St Cecilia. No surprise there. Alice chose St Roch, thereby bucking the trend of picking a saint of the same gender as yourself. St Roch, it turns out, is the patron saint of dogs and bad knees (sometimes the saints have to double up) and since Alice has both, it seemed to be more than a coincidence. Alex predictably saw this as a gauntlet thrown down.   While the rest of his catechism class were picking saint names from the usual suspects, Alex was after something altogether more unusual. Not for him the usual Premier league saints (St Mary, St Francis, St Theresa and so on). No, for Alex it had to be Praetextatus. That's right, Praetextatus. And don't pretend you've heard of him!

You can imagine the celestial waiting-room, with the saints waiting for their names to be called. "St Mary -- yes, St Joseph -- yes, St Mark -- you too, St John -- you're up" calls out Gabriel "and, hang on a minute, St Praetextatus". "Yes" shouts Praetextatus and punches the air. He doesn't get too many gigs.

That was Tuesday. And with Praetextatus metaphorically dusting down his top hat and tails, we just have to get Alex to the church on Sunday. Five days to go. Plain sailing. Or rather not. We haven't somehow factored in cricket on Wednesday. A mixup between Alex and another team member over a high catch sees Alex felled by a cricket ball to the head. Several rather anxious hours follow with Alex looking decidedly out of sorts and me agonising over whether this is shock, concussion or intracranial haemorrhage. Shock is easy -- sweet tea, sympathy and rest. Concussion might need a trip to the hospital and intracranial haemorrhage is a blue flash dash. Shining lights into his pupils is the conventional neurological assessment -- I've watched Casualty. Since I don't have a torch with me and the only sources of available light are the Jag's headlights, I decide to apply an entirely ad hoc neurological approach of my own devising. I suggest KFC on the way home. Suddenly Alex is Lazarus, raised from the dead and happily detailing which particular chicken combo might best address his medical needs. Miraculous recovery -- way to go Praetextatus!

We spend much of Wednesday night shining lights in Alex's eyes to check his pupils constrict equally. Much parental debate follows over what the response is meant to be. Alex, increasingly irritated by the hourly torchfest, suggests we might like to go to bed. Or watch Casualty until we know what we are doing. Thursday dawns, Alex is sent to school with an ibuprofen and Alice heads off to the stables. She shares a pony – Jemima – with a friend. Or more accurately we lease the pony. Three hours later I collect a monosyllabic Alice. She passes me a smashed mobile phone. "Jemima stood on my Blackberry" she tells me "twice". Alice waves away my attempts to mollify. "No Dad," says Alice "she is dogfood".

Saturday is cricket day with Alex with I donning our whites for the first time this season. The 4th XI opens its 2011 campaign with a victory, Alex scything through the opposition top order with exemplary swing bowling, and picking up his best ever bowling figures (4 for 13) en route. The skipper suggests I whack him over the head before every game. I am out for my second duck of the season and Alex generously suggests that perhaps my batting might usefully benefit from a blow to the head.

We reach Sunday mercifully without further mishap. Alex in a black shirt and M&M tie rehearses the bidding prayers. Despite the rather fabulous name, Praetextatus is not a major player. It's not clear even though there are any many miracles ascribed to him either, apart from the previous Wednesday's KFC resurrection. He seems to have rather drifted into sainthood. Even the Bishop, down from Southwark for the confirmations, has never heard of him and makes a hash of his name when reading it aloud. Not that the congregation knew any different.

As communion begins, Catherine frantically gestures for tissues. Despite my initial thoughts, Catherine has not been overcome by the solemnity of the occasion. Rather, Alex has picked this moment to have a nosebleed and he can hardly receive the Blood of Christ whilst dripping with blood like a lamb chop himself. Receiving the sacrament is one thing, becoming it is quite another. Alice comes to the rescue, extracting a wodge of tissues and elbowing her way through the communion queue as though it were the first day of the Harrods sale. Those years of combat-level retail therapy have not been wasted.

Three children, all of them confirmed, says Claire. Six grandchildren, says Nanna. Both are puffed with vicarious pride. I leave them chattering while I pour myself a whisky. A nod heavenward to Praetextatus.

"Cheers".

PRECIOUS
Sunday 15th May 2011

There's nothing quite like an incurable illness to focus your mind on what really matters in life. Faced with life's trials and tribulations, fixtures and fittings, pie and mash, you soon learn to recognise what is important and what is just parsley. For those unfortunate enough to have serious, sudden and terminal illnesses, it can be a pretty swift clear out. But for those lucky ones, if lucky is what I mean, with longer term illnesses, there is time to reflect a little while you focus on the meaningful. And when it comes to focusing your mind, I can't fault Parkinson's. It's absolutely top notch.

When it comes to shaking things into the dustbin of life, Parkinson's is your best mate. Just when I think I can't live without something, I find I can. Touchscreen computing for instance. Make no mistake I love my iPad. Couldn't live without it. Or so I thought. But as the tremors worsen, the iPad becomes a challenge (we Parkies do love to use the word challenge when what we actually mean is struggle). Words mistyped, buttons mispressed and so on. The Internet is the worst. You tap a hyperlink for the latest fajita recipe from Tesco and a misplaced tremor sends you spiralling onto a page about 18th century bookbinding techniques in St Petersburg. Exciting though that may be, it won't feed a family. Touchscreens take no prisoners. I'll just have to live without it. It's okay. Not a big deal.

Handwriting too. My tremor is now so bad that my handwriting is all but illegible. The bank queries cheques, handwritten letters are a thing of the past (not that I was ever the most diligent correspondent) and I have to ask the kids to write out the weekly shopping lists to prevent misunderstanding: Shaving cream, Radox and hairgel are poor substitutes, as I have discovered, for whipping cream, raspberries and meringue if you are making pavlova. Sure, it's frustrating to lose the ability to write. Five years ago, an inability to write would have been unimaginable. Now I can hardly remember what it was like. I just shrug my shoulders and move on. Wave goodbye to handwriting. I can live without it. It's okay. Not a big deal.

Cooking then. I have always enjoyed imaginative (for imaginative read experimental) cooking, taking a handful of improbable ingredients and weaving these into a melange of vibrant tastes. Slicing, chopping, mixing and stirring. All fine motor skills requiring precision, accuracy and strength, characteristics that have now gone on sabbatical. You could grow an onion in the time it takes me to slice one. Harvest crops in the time it takes me to peel a handful of potatoes. There is no fast food in our house. So the kids cook more as does Claire. It's not all bad -- I think the family are quietly relieved to be spared some of my more experimental recipes. Even for my family, there is a limit to how many times they can say "yes it's really quite nice" with anything that passes for conviction. They will just have to live without my cooking. It's okay. Not a big deal.

Cricket. As regular readers of this column will know, I play cricket at the weekends with my son Alex. Whilst Alex is an asset to the team, my contributions fall into the "embarrassing dad" category -- immaculate pristine whites, spanking new bat and fascination with statistics. Sadly my on field contributions are a little less valuable. Most innings are catching practice for the opposition fielders. The first season was fun, the learning experience shared by all the other members of the 4th XI. The second even more so, raising funds for the Cure Parkinson's Trust. With the third season just underway, I am having to face reality. I run like a Galapagos tortoise, throw like a two-year-old and bat with all the dazzling footwork of John Sargant. Whereas I was quietly and generously tolerated for the first couple of seasons, I think the joke is wearing thin. There is a queue of bright young players looking to play in the team, and probably wondering who the stiff at gully is. And they're right of course. Like a slow driver blocking the fast lane on a motorway, it's time to move aside. I started playing cricket again to play alongside Alex and that was precious. I suspect this will be his last season in the mighty 4ths, but for different reasons, probably moving on to higher teams. So the end of this season is probably a good time to bow out myself.

It's okay. Not a big deal.

THE FIERCE URGENCY OF NOW
Undated, May 2011

Parkinson's does not stand still. Every single hour of every single day it is quietly gnawing away at our nerve cells. Like mice in the attic, scurrying around, nibbling at cables. Little by little this gradual erosion takes away our future and even our present.

But only if we let it. If Parkinson's does not stand still, nor should we. We don't have to accept this gradual slow decline. Four decades ago there was no treatment. Prospects were grim. Levodopa changed that. Levodopa gave people who had no future cause for rejoicing. And we were grateful. Really grateful.

But that was forty years ago. It's hard to believe that in four decades of drug development, we have nothing to offer better than levodopa.

There are not many fields of medicine where the best drug available is forty years old. What should have been the dawning of a new age of pharmacotherapy for Parkinson's has turned out to be its high water mark.

And the mood of patients has changed. We were grateful forty years ago for levodopa. But that gratitude has been replaced by frustration and disappointment at the snail's pace of drug development that has followed. New, better treatments for Parkinson's are overdue. They were overdue thirty years ago if we are honest.

So next time you see a neurologist, ask him why the best drug he has to offer is forty years old. Ask him when there will be something better. Will we be celebrating the Golden Jubilee of levodopa before anything better is available?

When I was diagnosed with Parkinson's nearly five years ago, I was told glibly by my neurologist that a cure for Parkinson's was no more than ten years away. Sat next to me in the waiting room was a man who had Parkinson's for more than two decades, diagnosed in 1988. "You know what" he snorted "he told me the same thing".

SURVIVING CONFERENCES
Sunday 27th May 2011

In an idle moment yesterday afternoon, I calculated that I have attended some eighty international conferences in the time I've been in academia. At an average length of say four days and factoring in the odd day of travel, it transpires that I've spent just over a year of my life at a conference somewhere in the world. Monitoring molecules in Malaysia, dopamine in Dhaka, antidepressants in Ankara, psychiatry in Stockholm. Been there, done that, got the many T-shirts. Some are plush swanky affairs, with thousands (sometimes even tens of thousands) of delegates, based around gigantic conference centres the size of the Houston Astrodome. Others are cosy little affairs with a handful of like-minded scientists. Almost a fireside chat. To be honest they tend to blur into one. I can't remember the details of each.

But I have to say that conferences, especially international conferences, take a toll. Unfamiliar places, complex travel arrangements, taxi drivers who think they are Michael Schumacher and hotels built by Lego all serve to discombobulate the average itinerant neuroscientist. I don't know about you but I'm usually cream-crackered before I've even attended the scientific sessions.

And the pattern seems to be repeated wherever you are in the world. You arrive dishevelled at the hotel thrusting a handful of coins back into your pocket and trying to mentally translate the taxi fare from airport to hotel into pounds. By the time you've done so, the taxi is vanishing into the distance, and you realise that you could have bought a taxi for less. Actually you could have bought the aeroplane for less.

A quick shower then to the hotel bar where you run into an old friend you haven't seen in years. Then Werner's students arrive, knocking back vodka and Red Bull as though it is going out of fashion. You tag along when the group goes to the restaurant. It's late and the youngsters suggest a nightclub. You plead age and infirmity to no avail and before you know it, suddenly you're John Travolta on the dancefloor, rolling back the years to the horror of Werner's students, embarrassed to the point of disbelief. In a brief moment of insight, you decide to head back to the hotel. Time for a night cap in the bar. A voice calls your name -- it's Danny and suddenly it seems a brilliant idea to work your way alphabetically through the whiskies. I've never got beyond G but then there are an awful lot of Glensomethings to wade through. 2AM and several minutes of hammering on the door and fumbling with the key card entry system eventually succeeds in gaining entry to your room, but only after the entire corridor has been woken.

The following morning, kneeling over the toilet, the whisky tour seems a significantly less brilliant idea, your head feels as though it has been clamped in an industrial vice and your breath would bring down a charging rhinoceros. The morning scientific sessions start at 8:30 and you are clearly in no shape to attend. The Filipino chambermaid, arriving cheerily at 9:30, swiftly realises that the whimpering sounds from the bathroom are an infinitely more eloquent exhortation to leave the room untouched than the "do not disturb" hanging on the door handle.

Three hours later, blinking in the daylight, you emerge from the room to do battle with the scientific session. Shaving has not gone well -- tufts of stubble intermingle with tissue paper, like scarecrows over pimples scythed through by the blade, the entire dislocating effect somehow enhanced by the shaving foam behind your ears. Even the chambermaid, hedging her bets somewhat, ventures that "it's a lovely day outside, sir". Or, translated into English, "get out of this room so I can clean it". Werner and Danny are in the coffee shop, nursing cappuccinos and painkillers, while they peer over the conference program. Despite the nausea and blistering headache, the science is compelling. You resolve to attend the afternoon session, but only after more espresso.

And so the pattern repeats itself. Despite the best intentions in the world, you usually end up trashed on the first evening.

Self-discipline is everything in conferences so I have derived a series of rules to get you through that first crucial evening.

1)   Don't drink at all on the first evening of the conference. If you must, always keep the conference program with you to remind yourself why you are here in the first place.

2)   Avoid the temptation to tag along with large boozy groups of postgrads. Unless embarrassing yourself gives you a kick. It probably doesn't

3)   Do not attempt to dance when you've been drinking. Actually do not attempt to dance at all. Senior scientists doing The Time Warp is Youtube material. Don't go there.

4)   Drinking a glass of fine malt whisky is a life enhancing experience. Drinking five isn't.

5)   Just because the full English breakfast is included in your hotel room rate, don't feel you have to do it. A metabolism normally subjected to cornflakes will rebel.

There – easy when you know how...

June

It's June and D-day had dawned. That's D for DOPA, as in levodopa. Although I called it D day, I am not nervous. A progressive worsening of symptoms had taken me to the point where I know it is time to get on the train.

Many of us, myself included, put off taking levodopa for as long as possible. Maybe we fear the dyskinesias associated with long-term treatment, those helicopter movements that set you apart and embarrass friends. Maybe we believe that levodopa improves symptoms but only at the expense of faster decline? There is always a reason to procrastinate.

But eventually you run out of reasons to stall. You reach a place that the dopamine agonists can't go. You need something stronger. Then you are ready. But you have to reach that decision for yourself.

It's been 4½ years since I was diagnosed. I've spun it out as long as I could but now it's D-day.

And I'm ready.

WHO ARE YOU CALLING INCURABLE?
Undated, June 2011

One of the first things we learn about Parkinson's disease, rightly or wrongly, is that it is incurable.

Sometimes we learn that from our neurologist, sometimes from the Internet or other sources. But for all patients struggling to come to terms with the diagnosis, incurable is not a word we want to hear.

Keen to sugar an otherwise bitter pill, neurologists will often tell patients that Parkinson's is treatable. A range of treatments can keep the symptoms at bay for years.

So that's all right then.

Actually no. Current treatments will improve symptoms certainly. But they carry a price, for many a high price. Personality changes and a spectrum of nonmotor symptoms are the price we pay for keeping our bodies moving. And while the drugs keep us moving, we have time to reflect on that word incurable.

Why? Why is it incurable? Who says so?

So we do a little reading and, sooner or later, we wonder why Parkinson's should be different from any other condition. We can cure heart disease, some cancers and most infectious disease. So why not Parkinson's?

These are reasonable questions and before long we start to ask our neurologists the same questions: Doctor, why is there no cure for Parkinson's? And then our doctors talk to their colleagues and ask the same questions.

And little by little, the Parkinson's community begins to realise that there is nothing special about Parkinson's. It is a condition like any other. One by one the list of conditions that we can cure is lengthening. One by one, conditions are moved from the 'treatable' to the 'curable' column.

I've been working in the field of Parkinson's, as a researcher and latterly as a patient too, for more than twenty years and it is time that we acknowledge this seachange in thought. As a researcher, I expect to see a cure. As a patient, I demand it. We, the Parkinson's community, are no longer happy with 'treatable'. We have had enough of 'treatable'. We want 'curable'.

And we want it now.

WRITTEN IN THE STARS
Wednesday 8th June 2011

It looks as though I'm in a bit of a pickle. And it's all written in the stars. According to my old friend Tizer, who knows about these things, Venus is in opposition to Saturn in my seventh house for most of the latter part of the week. Well definitely until the weekend.

Bummer.

Tizer rubs his chin while he ponders a suitably convoluted 'clarification'.

Leaving aside the fact that I barely own the house we live in let alone a seventh house, Tizer's arm flailing explanation is not good news. And all because of Venus and Saturn. You know, Saturn, the big fella with the rings?

Saturn is pretty much the daddy of the planets, certainly not somebody to mess with. An enforcer in dark glasses. If Ray Winstone were a planet, he would be Saturn. Now Venus on the other hand, is a bit of a girly. All glittery jewellery and the latest fluffy fashions. Sort of Keira Knightley perhaps? But let's face it, if it comes to fisticuffs, she's not going to be much of a match for Ray.

Venus couldn't knock the skin off a rice pudding so we're going to need some celestial muscle. As luck would have it, it turns out that Mars is pretty close to Jupiter this week. Which is news to me because only last week they were bickering like an old married couple. You can't turn your back for a minute -- one second they're squabbling, the next they are best mates.

But you can't always pick your friends. So if we need Mars and Jupiter to give Venus a bit of backup, so be it. Mars, being pretty much the god of war, is the sort of planet you want on your side. If there's a ruck, you can be pretty sure that Mars will be somewhere in the middle of it. A sort of planetary Gareth Chilcott. And Jupiter is one of those guys who will never say no to a good time. A combination of Oliver Reed and Brian Blessed, with a huge thirst for life.

So it's Keira Knightley, Gareth Chilcott and Oliver-Brian Blessed-Reed against Ray Winstone in a sort of astrological shootout. And that's without Mercury moving in recession. Well aren't we all.

Too close to call? Well it all depends on your star sign says Tizer. I'm a Libra. According to Tizer, that makes me diplomatic and urbane in a sort of Graham Greene colonial way. I am also romantic and charming. Apparently. Not to mention easygoing and sociable, all of which paints me as a cross between Michael Parkinson and George Clooney. And when you add in the fact that I am idealistic and peaceable, I could be Mother Teresa. Just as I'm beginning to warm to Tizer's appraisal of my warm avuncular nature, he let slip that there is a downside. I'm also not only indecisive and changeable (I don't agree, well maybe he's got a point), but gullible and easily influenced, flirtatious and self-indulgent. This is the last time I invite Tizer over for a drink I am thinking. Don't you bandy planets with me.

What does this mean I ask Tizer, keen to draw a line under this character assassination. Apparently I shouldn't leave anything to chance on the 12th, because I'm wiser and more experienced by the 14th, should ride my luck on the 16th, tell an old friend that enough is enough on the 17th, and see life through a different perspective on the 19th.

Oh yes, I nearly forgot – I will meet a tall dark handsome stranger on the 20th. I imagine that'll be the estate agent with the deeds to my seventh house.

SKIPPER
Saturday 11th June 2011

For reasons that are generous but entirely unfathomable, at least to me, the last few Saturdays have found me not only playing cricket, but captain of our club's 4th XI.

The Bells Yew Green 4th XI is a team in transition. When founded a couple of years ago we were, and the others won't mind me saying so, a team of limitless enthusiasm tempered by rather more limited ability. The initial idea was to have a dads and lads team where sons would learn from fathers, while fathers would proudly watch sons develop into mature cricketers. This laudable objective lasted perhaps two games into the inaugural season. We very swiftly realised two things. Firstly that we didn't really have enough father-son combinations to fill a team and secondly, where we did, the sons were, for the most part, better cricketers than the fathers. So although there were any number of dads, even grandads, and lads in the team, there were comparatively few genetic matches.

It also soon became apparent that we were virtually the only team playing to this rather quaint paternalistic ethos. Most of the opposition teams we faced were entirely composed of adults. Moreover they tended to be strong muscular adults who had played at county level, or were capable of hitting the ball into the next county. Not surprisingly, they feasted on our twelve year old bowlers like crocodiles at a water hole.

On the rare occasions we played teams with any fathers and sons, they tended to be all fathers, uncles, sons and cousins. In one case, and no I shan't name the village, the entire team appeared to be the product, as far as one could tell, of a single genome. Not so much a gene pool as a gene puddle. Faced with this kind of negative biodiversity in some of these more remote Sussex villages, you can't help but conclude that they don't get out much. There is nothing quite so unsettling as batting in front of a slip cordon of four seemingly identical, gap toothed, unshaven skinheads. I swear I could hear banjo music.

Our 2009 and 2010 campaigns were largely a catalogue of defeats. Games followed a fixed pattern. Inevitably we lose the toss and the opposition skipper asks us to field for 50 overs in Saharan heat while the opposition batting sends us scurrying to every part of the field. They declare on 300 and tuck into the sandwiches with similar zeal. Our dehydrated openers last less than an over and suddenly our youngsters are exposed to a West Indian fast bowler who is clearly intent on singlehandedly filling the local A&E department. As balls whistle past ears, the match begins to look like a seal cull. The ambulances keep their engines running.

Loss followed dispiriting loss and despite some brave performances with bat and ball, the 4th XI always found itself struggling. In the first season we escaped relegation by the width of a cigarette paper. In the second season we were less lucky, finishing last and tumbling ignominiously into Division 13, the Bermuda Triangle of the East Sussex Cricket League. Mercifully the flatulent, grunting Sussex Neanderthals secured promotion.

So a new beginning for the 4th XI in 2011 and I'm delighted to say that we are doing really rather well. In fact better than that, we are top of the league, having won four of five matches, albeit often by nailbitingly close margins. Some habits die hard and, as we know from bitter experience, there is no position so secure that the 4th XI, cannot snatch defeat from the jaws of victory. No opening stand large enough that it cannot be negated by a batting collapse of biblical proportions. But despite these acknowledged batting frailties, we have still scraped home. For four of those five matches, I have been the skipper. And nobody is more surprised than me. The first week, I was delighted and honoured to be asked. By the fourth, I was beginning to wonder if things were that bad with the 4th XI that a 53-year-old man with Parkinson's and no natural cricketing ability is the preferred choice as captain.

Of course the role of captain in the 13th division of the East Sussex Cricket League is some way removed from anything that Andrew Strauss might be expected to undertake. Strauss has nothing more complicated to occupy his mind than field placings and bowler rotation. The absence of juniors in the England team also means that Strauss does not have to fret over Under 15 bowlers exceeding their six over quota or accidentally fielding closer than eleven yards from the batsmen. Nor does he wake up in a cold sweat over collecting match fees, or whose name is next on the tea rota. And then there is always the young seamer allergic to flour and therefore liable to keel over at the mere sight of a custard cream wafted under his nose. These are weighty matters and the skipper who ignores them does so at his peril.

On-field duties are, in comparison, a doddle. A few magisterial waves of the arm to move fielders and the odd word of encouragement to the bowlers seem to cover it. If one of the fielders takes a catch, you look like a tactical wizard. Having said that, there can be some tricky moments. Telling Graeme Swann that he is not needed to bowl is one thing. Say the same to an already grumpy twelve-year-old and you will see the word petulance defined with a level of clarity that makes the OED's effort seem an exercise in obfuscation. Graeme Swann will take it on the chin. In the 4th XI, the captain is more likely to get it on the chin.

Then there are the supporters. A crowd of thirty thousand will pack Lords on a test match day. At our home fixtures we are lucky to get ten. Counting the dogs. And the scorers. And half of these have gone to the wrong game. Dogs and children chasing balls on the outfield are minor irritations. But nothing beats the occasion our fielding was distracted by two topless sunbathers on the deep mid-wicket boundary. Before your imagination runs away with you, I should say that both were tattooed and the size of walruses. As if their mere presence was not intimidation enough, they spent the afternoon taunting our young fielders. Some, like soldiers returning from the Somme, still bear the psychological scars. One has developed a stammer. Even the batsmen asked for the sightscreen to be moved.

OOH I SAY!
Tuesday 21st June 2011

It was nearly nine o'clock in the evening, under the floodlit roof of Wimbledon's Centre Court, when Andy Murray finally dispatched some hapless Frenchman whose name eludes me, the poor fellow unlucky enough to have drawn the local favourite in the first round of this year's Wimbledon. Despite winning fifteen games on the trot, Murray had given us the usual worries by needlessly dropping the first set. Still, it wouldn't be Wimbledon otherwise.

I have to confess that it's been a long time since I've seriously watched tennis. Decades in fact. I can remember the very first Wimbledon I saw on television, in 1973, with Billie Jean King dismissing Chris Evert in the ladies final with ruthless efficiency. And although Mrs King was unequivocally the better player, it was Chris Evert who, understandably, made the greater impression on the fifteen-year-old Jon.

Whilst the ladies played a version of tennis that even I could understand, with its rallies and skill, the men's game appeared to have evolved in an entirely different direction, with a serve and volley approach becoming more commonplace. To me that seemed to strip the game of its beauty and reduce it to a thing of cynical brutality. All emphasis was on a first serve of blistering speed. And no player distilled that ethos more than Roscoe Tanner, a country boy from Lookout Mountain in Tennessee who served at 150 mph. Not surprisingly a good many of his first serves were aces, whistling past his opponent's ears and leaving him dazed and bewildered. But nowhere near as bewildered as Tanner himself if his opponent actually returned the ball. Which wasn't often. Although one admired Tanner's sheer power, it didn't make for much of a spectator sport. Gradually, the male players became increasingly robotic -- Bjorn Borg, Ivan Lendl and even the irascible John McEnroe. It wasn't the temper tantrums that turned me off tennis. It was the tennis itself. There seemed to be a long period when power trumped skill.

So for many decades, I did little more than catch the highlights on television, watching the hordes queue in the seemingly inevitable rain of Wimbledon fortnight, railing against the price of strawberries which seems each year to be measured in Krugerrands. If the match looked particularly engaging, I might watch the ladies or men's final. Especially if there was a British interest which was, let's face it, about as frequent as total solar eclipses. Like most of the nation I was glued to a black-and-white television in 1977 when Virginia Wade won it in Jubilee year. Not only a popular winner but a local girl to boot! There hasn't been a male winner in my lifetime. Fred Perry in 1936 was the last, before television more or less.

But yesterday was rather different. No highlights on television for us yesterday. Yesterday was the real deal. Because Anton and Freia had four tickets, a fabulous

168

surprise from Freia's aunt Susan, a former player and member at Wimbledon. And not just any tickets mind you -- Centre Court no less.

And, being Susan's guests, we had the run of the members' enclosure. And the contrast with TV coverage could not be more pronounced. Television gives no sense of the spectacle. No sense of the drama. No sense of the excitement of actually being on Centre Court. Or of watching Nadal or Murray, as we did yesterday. Nor does television capture all the business of Wimbledon, the smart suits, posh frocks and colourful characters.

Just for a day, we got into our glad rags and rubbed shoulders with the glitterati of the tennis world, sipping Pimms as Susan, a regular at Wimbledon since 1946, pointed out former players and champions, fleshing out each with anecdotes and stories. You couldn't wish for a better host. And I did my homework -- determined not to look a complete chump, I made sure I knew the names of all the current players, their rankings and so forth. Like a Bateman cartoon, the members' enclosure is not the place to confess that you don't know who is who on the circuit.

On Centre Court we watched the champion, Rafael Nadal begin his defence with a composed straight sets victory, assertive without being arrogant, confident but not cocky. He will be hard to beat. And even when the rains came, as come they must at Wimbledon, we sheltered in the members enclosure and whiled away the interruption with clotted cream and jam scones as they closed the roof on Centre Court in preparation for the evening spectacle, when Andy Murray began his 2011 challenge. Initially hesitant, he visibly grew in confidence, winning both of the last two sets 6-0. The contrast in style with Nadal could not be clearer. The subtle weighted shots of Murray or the raw blistering power of Nadal. If the seeding follows its prescribed course, these two are destined to meet in the semi-final and I cannot escape the feeling that we saw the 2011 Wimbledon champion yesterday in Murray or Nadal.

Of course the next two weeks will prove me right or wrong. But I'll tell you one thing that will be different about this Wimbledon for me - I shall be glued to the TV for the next two weeks.

Do not disturb.

PHOEBE
Monday 27th June 2011

Let me tell you about an artist, and what she taught me about art and life. And unknowingly too because we never met. And what she taught me was in many ways unrelated to art.

Artistic creativity is one of the more bizarre side-effects of Parkinson's and/or the medications we endure. Not, as you can imagine, a side-effect that many of us would complain about. Constipation, blurred vision and aches and pains may send us scurrying to our doctors for relief. But not many of us buttonhole our physicians about art.

"You see Doc, it's a bit embarrassing -- I've turned into Van Gogh. One minute I'm giving the living room ceiling a second coat of eggshell blue emulsion, then suddenly I come over all starry night. It's driving the wife crazy. And she says the sunflowers make her sneeze".

Each year for the last decade Parkinson's UK has run a competition for art, photography, poetry and, latterly, digital art. The Mervyn Peake awards, set up in celebration of the famous illustrator and author of Gormenghast, reflect Peake's struggle with Parkinson's and attract hundreds of entries each year. I have been fortunate enough to win the photography award a few years ago and have been commended for paintings and photography in other years.

But when it comes to art, I have to admit to having a bit of a head start. Art runs in the family. Whilst my father's ancestors were farmers and railwaymen, many of my ancestors on my mother's side were artists. When I say 'artists' I mean painters of course. Victorians from the mill towns of Lancashire and Yorkshire would have no truck with other 'modern' art forms. This was the world of Atkinson Grimshaw and Tissot.

As a child it seemed that every adult in my family painted. My aunts and uncles would knock off a few daubs in their spare time, and faded photographs of their parents, standing optimistically by easels, peered through the fog of generations in family albums. Every time I admired a picture on the wall, it turned out to be the work of one or other ancestor, gothic figures from another time.

Spanning those generations, linking the quick and the dead, was my grandmother and her sisters. And I have written before of the mornings spent in my grandmother's company when I was a child. Her sisters Ivy and Cicely painted too. But none of my artist relatives inspire me more than my grandmother's older sister, my great aunt Phoebe, born in Scarborough in 1893. Of all the painting sisters, Phoebe was special. Despite growing up in North

Yorkshire, between Scarborough and Hebden Bridge, with no formal artistic training to my knowledge, she somehow unearthed a significant talent for painting. Of all the sisters, Phoebe impressed me most. Not because she exhibited at the Royal Academy, although she did. Not because she was a talented photographer either, which she was. But because she had a zest for life, a need to create. The name Phoebe is derived from the Greek, and means *the shining one*. Never was a name more appropriate.

All we have left of Phoebe is a handful of papers, a few paintings and two sepia photographs. The first shows Phoebe, as a pre-Raphaelite figure with long corkscrew curls and deep soulful eyes. A woman of confidence and a deep artistic sensitivity, determined to follow her muse wherever it led. The photograph was taken around 1916 in Blackpool. A young woman, looking forward on life and determined to enjoy everything that life had to offer. "Carpe Diem" she might have said "seize the day".

The second photograph taken five years later shows a frail tentative shadow of the same woman, her lungs ravaged by tuberculosis Phoebe left England on 3rd November 1922 for South Africa, in the hope that the warm climate might aid convalescence. She died on the voyage. She was 29.

The light that burns twice as bright burns half as long.

So what lessons does a 29-year-old artist have for a 53-year-old Parkie? Simple -- live life to the full. Phoebe lived life to the full. And into her short life she crammed so many achievements, so much to be proud of, and so many memories for her friends and family. She lived each day not as though it were her last, but as if it was her first, her sense of wonder undimmed.

Phoebe truly seized the day.

July

I've made a tough decision – this will be my last season playing cricket. I do not take this decision lightly, recognising in its import another victory of the Parkinson's over me. I prefer to think of it as an awakening of reality. I can no longer throw the ball and my reactions are perceptibly slower. I can hardly run. My batting, always scratchy, has withered to nothing – the ball comes on to me much faster. It strikes me as often as the bat. Each week is a litany of bruises. Serious injury is a genuine risk.

But I'm not despondent – I'm thankful. Thankful for these three summers playing alongside Alex and watching him grow as a cricketer. Thankful for letting me be a proud father. Thankful for this final swansong with the game I love. Thankful to the Parkinson's for making me play, for not putting it off, for making me seize the day.

In sport, they say you know when it's time to call it a day. I do and it is.

THUNDER
Monday 4th July 2011

It all depended who you asked. If I asked my father what thunder was, a long and detailed description about charge and discharge would follow. Fully accurate, I'm sure, but nonetheless a level of detail well beyond the ken of a seven-year-old. The same question put to my mother was brushed aside with "It's God moving his furniture". I remember thinking at the time that, if that was the case, the Almighty was pretty clumsy. It worried me. Every thunderclap had me looking skyward for signs of celestial pianos crashing earthward or broken heavenly table legs or mattresses. In any case, why did the Almighty pick a thunderstorm as a cue to rearrange interior decor?

Eddie Franks, of inordinately scatological leaning even for a seven-year-old, said that thunder was the sound of God breaking wind, and that rain was therefore ... well, you know. He expressed it in rather more fulsome, and infinitely more profane language. This oblique theological stance may go some way towards explaining why Eddie Franks was the only boy ever to be expelled from communion class. The vicar even murmured darkly about exorcism.

But from as far back as I can remember, I've always been fascinated by thunderstorms. Whilst a night-time storm would send my sister scurrying into my parents' bed for comfort, I would throw back the curtains and open the windows. It didn't matter that the rain was lashing the windowsill like the scene on the heath in King Lear, I would do anything to get closer to the storm. Nothing thrilled me more than the sight of fork lightning and the excited counting. Was the storm approaching or receding? Sometimes storms would pass by innocuously along the Don Valley, rumbling and grumbling, flashing and forking as they went. But every once in awhile, the storm would change direction and turn menacingly towards us until thunder and lightning were exactly synchronised, the storm directly overhead. Sometimes it even drowned out my sister's shrieks and whimpers. Sometimes.

When I worked in America I witnessed amazing storms that would rumble like juggernauts across the great plains, the skies lit like daylight by the constant lightning, swirling winds bringing flash floods that turned baked fields into mud. Somehow America always seemed to be a country of weather extremes. Whilst hail might be the size of grapeshot in Britain, hail stones the size of baseballs would fall in America. Hail that could kill. We have had one UK hurricane in 30 years. In America they are annual occurrences. Our little hurricane caused power cuts and brought down trees and slates while Katrina, like some avenging angel, turned New Orleans into a scene from a Mad Max movie as civilisation disintegrated and America stood, like a rabbit in the headlights, seemingly powerless to intervene.

In this country our relationship with the weather is usually more comfortable. Constable painted fluffy cumulus clouds on blue skies, temperate gentle weather from a benign Maker. Only Turner saw the weather for what it was capable of, painting ships foundering in squalls, malevolent tempests whipping up white horses and ships bobbing helplessly in gales.

Nowadays a good thunderstorm has me reaching for my CD collection. Somehow a thunderstorm needs musical accompaniment and Wagner seems to fit the bill. There is nothing quite like listening to the Ride of the Valkyries as the lightning flashes around you, conducting your imaginary orchestra. Even the neighbours have grown used to the shrieks and whoops of the Valkyries emanating from our house during a thunderstorm. Just another of Jon's quirks, they feel. Best say nothing.

But even so, thunder has a habit of making you a child again. No matter how much you know about charge and discharge, a thunderstorm can still serve as a reminder of who is The Boss. On Thursday, as the storms rumbled up the Rother valley, we were treated to an apocalyptic thunderstorm, rain overflowing the storm drains and testing the car's always questionable sunroof seals to destruction. As I slammed the front door behind me, a colossal thunderclap and lightning flash rattled the windows, tripped the fuses here and plunged the house into darkness.

I tell you I nearly wet myself.

OWZAT
Sunday 10th July 2011

Some British sporting events are of such global significance that they are on the lips of the entire country. If asked for a list, the man in the street might name Wimbledon, the FA Cup final, the British Grand Prix, or perhaps the Olympics. To this august list, I would like to suggest an addendum -- an annual cricketing spectacular featuring a glittering array of batting and bowling talent. The event of which I speak, and I'm sure you've all guessed by now, is the annual Bells Yew Green 3rd versus 4th XI clash. Gosh, I hear you say, has that come around again so quickly? Each year the 3rd XI captain has to face the 4th XI in a fixture where there is frankly nothing to gain and everything to lose.

Last year's game is the stuff of legends. Although the 3rd XI technically won the game last year, the 4th XI excelled in other cricketing areas, specifically sledging and ball tampering. They also ate more sandwiches. But, as they say, you cannot beat the 4th XI. You can only score more runs than them.

So this year Pete, James, Vish, John, Will, Huw, Tim, Joe, Guy, Callum, Iain, Harry, Tom, Nirav, Tarif, Keith, Paul and Chris joined the fun as Tarif's Knightriders fought Jon's Joyriders for this year's 3rd versus 4th XI bragging rights.

There are, as cricket nerds amongst you know, 11 different means by which batsmen may be dismissed. Bowled, caught, stumped and LBW are perhaps the most common. Batsmen may also be run out or even timed out, if they fail to reach the crease within three minutes of the fall the previous wicket. Obstructing the field is a curiosity, a dismissal hardly ever encountered in club cricket. In fact I've only seen it once -- in last year's 3rd versus 4th XI game. Opinion is divided on the legitimacy of the decision in this particular case but, as we are all widely taught, the umpire's decision is final and Out is Out.

And, whilst the outbound walk from pavilion to the crease seems short, buoyed by adrenaline and expectation, the same cannot be said of the return journey. The walk from crease to pavilion, inevitably tainted by disappointment, is of course a valuable time for reflection, an opportunity for mature contemplation and adjustment to the umpire's decision. In those eighty yards, disappointment becomes zen-like acceptance, commonly expressed in the form of a shake of the head or, as in this case, a series of sharp kicks to the wooden pavilion door. The marks on the pavilion door bear silent testimony to the encounter.

You learn much about people by their response to dismissal. In the course of yesterday's encounter, some 35 wickets fell and, whilst we (and the pavilion door) were spared the sound of boot on timber, there were a few slightly disappointed souls. Myself included. In the first innings, I lasted a mere two deliveries. The first I defended. The second I clipped directly to mid-wicket. No run. A fraction of a second later after a bloodcurdling call of YYYYYEEEEEESSSSSS from Julian, expressed with all the volume and ferocity of an Apache warcry, I was aware that I was no longer the sole batsmen at my end. Not expecting company, I set off. Even accounting for a couple of misfields, I was yards short. As I trudged off, I accepted my lot with poise, dignity and calm. And decided that Julian could damn well keep wicket for the afternoon.

My second innings was even shorter -- dismissed LBW to a first ball yorker -- in the process giving Joe a hat-trick and sending me hobbling back to the pavilion with a suspected broken toe. Including mine (dismissals that is, not broken toes) there were a grand total of 9 ducks, more than a Peking restaurant. In fact there were 25 single figure scores in an afternoon where the ball was in firm ascendancy over the bat.

There were some pretty impressive performances though. A hat-trick for Joe would normally give him the bragging rights over his dad. Except on a day when Tim scored 40 not out, clubbing the ball all around the park -- well, in the space behind square leg anyway. And Pete outscored his son James. Two nil to the dads on batting.

Bowling was a different picture with Joe and Harry walking roughshod over Tim and Chris. And as for fielding, it was almost a one-man show as the only person to distinguish himself yesterday afternoon was -- you've guessed it -- Julian, who took three superb catches as well as a sharp stumping. Proving once again that you can't keep a good man down!

On the whole, sledging is to be abhorred in cricket. In this fixture it is almost mandatory. It's hardly the mental disintegration of Steve Waugh's Australian teams. But there is a certain pleasure to be taken in having the slips make a batsman laugh so hard that they cannot focus on the fast bowler steaming in towards them. And when a son bowls to his father, he has to think carefully whether the pleasure of taking a wicket will be outweighed by the inevitable loss of pocket money that follows. As surely as night follows day.

In the end, the scores are irrelevant. It's off to the Brecknock, as the sun sets. Elsewhere, the 1st and 2nd XIs have won against tough opposition and the mood is relaxed as people talk of heroic feats of batting and bowling, of glorious catches and shocking dismissals. After a pint of Harvey's, nobody cares who scored what, who bowled who, or even what the results were. After several pints, nobody even remembers.

WEAPON OF CHOICE
Thursday 14th July 2011

Craft was the rather patronising catchall term used to describe everything that was timetabled on a Wednesday afternoon but was not fine art. This included printing, pottery and carpentry. Mr Murray's carpentry classes took place once a week in a long workshop shared with the pottery class. The air, a haze of sawdust, always smelt faintly of burning. Hardly surprising in a room where generations of adolescent boys consistently used ludicrously overpowered and inappropriate tools on native and imported hardwoods. Mr Murray never tired of telling us that carpentry was less about tools than about imagination, an exhortation embraced by some more than others. To this day I have never forgotten the sight of Burgess Minor firing up what appeared to be a petrol-driven chainsaw for his designated Lent term project -- a pair of speaker cabinets. Whilst most produced cabinets of fruit box dimensions, his were the size of Stonehenge. His father had to hire a Transit to get them home at the end of term.

The school prided itself on its wood workshops, boldly assuring us that, cost permitting, one could work any kind of wood. For the most part, students used oak, pine or plywood (there was no MDF in those days), sensible workaday woods for workaday projects. Occasionally Freddie Sopwith, self appointed class comedian, would suggest that their proposed third year letter rack project could only possibly be executed in seasoned ebony, rare Formosan teak or satinised English pear wood. Mr Murray would sigh and suggest that Mr Sopwith might like to reflect on the helpfulness of his suggestion while he, Mr Murray, honed an appropriate text for the hundred or so lines that would now fill Mr Sopwith's Saturday evening "I will not waste Mr Murray's valuable time with facetious requests for expensive woods that I know perfectly well my father cannot afford on a bus conductor's wages". Mr Murray was as skilful with troublemakers as he was with the lathe.

Although Mr Murray was the kind of teacher who made an indelible impression, his carpentry class somehow left me with no woodworking skills whatsoever. What it did do however was stir an interest in power tools that remains undimmed to this day. Specifically tools that make needlessly loud noises or require the user to wear protective equipment. Tools that sit uneasily at that interface between power and danger.

Of course that interface has shifted for me over the last few years. As Parkinson's has tightened its malign grip on my musculature, more tools cross that boundary from "noisy, powerful and fun" to "downright dangerous". A chainsaw in the hands of a skilled lumberjack is a perfect marriage of man and machine. The same tool, wielded by a 53 year-old Madopar-fuelled incompetent with akinesia and tremors begins to look like a trailer for a DIY home amputation video.

Of course all successful DIY is a result of having the correct tools to hand. Except for me. As Claire would freely tell you, I have a habit of buying a tool first and dreaming up a use later. This certainly applied to the staple gun, a tool of mouthwatering power but limited usage. For a week after I bought it, there was no upholstery, carpeting or furniture left untouched as me and the gun set about the house with a zeal that, try as I may, I never seem able to bring to housework. When I discovered that it would fire staples the length of the garden, DIY soon gave way to coke can target practice and then to deadheading the chrysanthemums.

The jigsaw was even better. Hardly a day passed without a piece of wood or MDF being subjected to its tender mercies. A parade of gloopy Dali-esque picture frames, table tops and boxes all bore witness to my love affair with the jigsaw and its wavy lines. Only when spotted by Claire marking up the patio table did the jigsaw honeymoon come to an end with an abrupt confiscation.

Another discreet trip to Homebase and I was suddenly the proud owner of a tile cutter. Despite the relatively task-specific name, I was quick to discover that this too was a tool of much wider applicability. And with a diamond blade, there is little that will not succumb to its incisive power. Still, I have to concede that my home made range of glass tableware, fashioned entirely from bottles has however remained stubbornly unpopular.

But my weapon of choice will always be the power washer. Never did the name of the product so dramatically undersell its capabilities. For washing the car, clearing the patio or demossing the roofing tiles, you can't beat it. But let your imagination run wild and before you know it, you have a new means of shooing cats from the garden, or welcoming Jehovah's Witnesses. So much fun, so little time.

It's all a case of using a bit of imagination. Just because a tool calls itself a tile cutter or orbital sander, don't let that inhibit you. In the right, or should I say wrong, hands the capacity for power-driven creative mayhem is endless. Think of Burgess Minor and his chainsaw. You'd never believe that he went on to be a neurosurgeon. And you know the best part -- I think Mr Murray would have approved.

PISCATORIAL PROCLIVITIES
Wednesday 20th July 2011

Many years ago we kept tropical fish, a pastime predicated on the view that watching the tank would be a relaxing experience at the end of a day of commuting. Listening to its soft bubbling and watching the fish glide aimlessly by should be the perfect antidote to the hustle and bustle of a Connex commuter train. A microcosm of tranquillity in a busy world. We stocked the tank with every kind of fish. You name it, we had it. Tetras, platys, guppies, loaches, gouramis, and so on, each a colourful little aquatic jewel. And each specifically chosen for their colour, size or shape. A rainbow nation of fish.

It sounded utopian and, in many respects, was. Because, as any fishkeeper will tell you, fish must be carefully chosen to be compatible with the other tank tenants. But for us, unlike many more informed and thus responsible tropical fish owners, the selection of fish for purely aesthetic qualities outweighed any compatibility issues. Instead of a happy piscatorial community, we had the aquatic equivalent of Big Brother. It mattered not one jot to us that the fishkeeping manual might describe a fish as "apt to sulk" or "not a community fish" or, most damningly explicit of all, "volatile and aggressive". No matter how stark the warning, we ignored it. If it looked good, in it went. For us, the coral pink gouramis went well with that iridescent purple cichlid. Sadly the cichlid felt that the gouramis went well with a nice Chianti.

And therein lies the problem. The most colourful fish are ironically the most vulnerable. An electric blue and red male cardinal tetra is thus coloured to attract a mate.

Sadly these same features also attract the attention of other less welcoming fish. Fish with large mouths, sharp teeth and different but equally compelling appetites. In those circumstances, being a piscine Ballesha Beacon turns out to be a poor evolutionary choice.

Sometimes the culprits were obvious, aggressively snacking on each other's fins in broad daylight. Others were stealthier, only showing their true colours at night. For a fortnight after we stocked the tank with fantailed guppies, their numbers would decrease by one each night. It was like an aquatic Agatha Christie. Only after a week did we put two and two together and make the association between the guppy attrition and the suddenly rather chubby catfish under the bridge. During daylight Tiddles was all sweetness and light but, the moment night fell, it became a voracious predator, setting about the guppies like a great white shark in miniature. Friends had a similar problem. The fish shop's reply when they voiced their concerns "Yeah, he can handle himself" was not reassuring.

Of course some fish are fairly obvious troublemakers. As you might imagine, a Siamese fighting fish is not a shy recluse. Apt to take a nip at most other tankdwellers, they are more than a mite tetchy. More than one in a tank and they kick off like a family of scousers. The clue is in the name. But others were less obvious, feigning 'Who? Me?' innocence before devouring all and sundry. Hannibal Lecter with scales.

It's fair to say that this does not make for a relaxing experience. Each evening, after a tiring day at work, we would come home to an aquatic version of the killing fields. Or south central Los Angeles. Each morning the children would anxiously count the fish and report the night's losses to us. Although a potent illustration of the cycle of life and death, that wasn't why we had the tank. And finding fish in fractions rather than integers upset the kids too.

Eventually we were left with Tiddles, smiling beatifically from beneath the bridge. A chastening experience. But two years of tropical fishkeeping at least allowed me to draw certain conclusions

1)   A tropical fish tank is about as relaxing as watching CCTV footage of Toxteth on a Saturday night.

2) On the whole, big fish eat little fish. Moreover big fish get to be big fish by eating little fish. A lot of them.

3)   Fish with the word 'fighting' in their name are best avoided.

4)   If fellow fishkeepers offer you fish, ask yourself why they are suddenly so keen to be rid of 'Fang' or 'Jaws'.

But the best solution is to buy an iPad and install the aquarium app. The fish swim slowly and gently from side to side. None of them bite the heads off each other. Nor are there pieces of dead fish floating on the top of the water. And you don't even have to feed them.

On the whole I've come to the conclusion that the best place for real fish is either in their natural habitat or wrapped in newspaper with a portion of chips. Either way, in an environment or a condition where they can squabble as much as they like -- I don't have to watch them.

It took me several years, but in the end I finally realised the truth -- fish are mindless sociopaths.

LOUIS AND AMY
Sunday 24th July 2011

This Friday gone had a bit of a musical theme. Catherine, as I think I have mentioned before, is a music student at a London conservatoire. Sounds awfully posh but the truth is that, for three terms a year, it means many hours a day of gruelling practice on the bassoon, an instrument she cheerfully describes as 'a log with jewellery'.

The upside of all these hours spent on staircase scales and swooping arpeggios is that Catherine and her jewelled log are much in demand for music courses and concerts over the summer. No sooner had she returned from a wind band tour to the Far East than she was summoned to an orchestral course in the West Country.

The culmination of this course was to be a concert in Wells cathedral of a couple of big classical barnstormers (Stravinsky's Rite of Spring and Tchaikovsky's fifth symphony). If that wasn't enticing enough, there was also to be a world premiere of a new violin concerto. Needless to say, Shop Till You Drop Alice and Xbox Alex could barely contain their indifference to this musical soiree. They had 'other plans' for the evening which, as far as I could tell, revolved around acres of Domino's pizza, gallons of glow-in- the-dark fizzy drinks and a Harry Potter video. Oh to be young.

But Catherine was keen that Claire and I attend the concert. Although initially touched by this gesture, it soon became apparent that our necessary presence had as much to do with providing a viable and cheap means of getting Catherine, bassoon and boyfriend Andrew home to

Kent. With the concert scheduled to finish at ten, and thanks largely to the tender ministries of Mr Beeching, there was no combination of trains and buses that would deliver Catherine to our doorstep much before Saturday afternoon. So at a little after two on Friday, I found myself on the M25 heading for Wells. Two hours later I was still on the M25, the normal Friday afternoon getaway further swelled on this weekend by holiday traffic.

The rest of the journey was a blur of espresso, diesel fumes and Stonehenge until eventually, around half past six, I pulled up in a Wells car park, bursting for a toilet. One of the lesser joys of Parkinson's is urgency, a small word that barely hints at the kind of panicked 'I need a pee NOW' sentiments I thought I had left behind in childhood. Wells is clearly a cultured city - the car park toilets were not only impeccably clean, but also resonated to piped music, in this case in the form of The Ride of the Valkyries. I kid you not.

Catherine was waiting on the lawn outside the cathedral along with boyf Andrew, a composer of impenetrably complex orchestral pieces but with an engaging weakness for obscure cheeses. The orchestral course had, it transpired, been a rather boozy affair with the course fee being spent more on beer than bedrooms. This ethos had extended to the concert and, although the sherry-sipping girls in the strings were on top of their game, we should not expect much sense from the thirstier sections of the orchestra. Boat races and brass instruments, say no more. Certainly they had put the time between final rehearsal and performance to good use.

After a brief mixup over seating – a rather fractious steward keen to eject the Kent interlopers in favour of the local glitterati who had doublebooked our seats – the audience were given a brief welcome from the rector who assured us that we would enjoy the musical feast before us. Presumably he knew nothing of The Rite of Spring or would not have so cheerily endorsed a musical depiction of pagan fertility dances, tribal wars and virgin sacrifices.

For those of you who do not know Stravinsky's work, there is a disarmingly large amount of percussion and it's fair to say that what the kitchen department lacked in accuracy was compensated by enthusiasm. No prizes for guessing the winners of the highest bar bill for the week. Mercifully their exuberance successfully masked my principal indiscretion of the evening, failing to switch off my Blackberry, a crime that went mostly unnoticed only because reception in the cathedral was so sketchy. Or because I have no friends. Still, as indiscretions go, that was probably trumped by my evening somnolence, briefly falling asleep on the shoulder of the man in seat E13.

The violin concerto was cancelled because the soloist was apparently unwell although rumour abounded that the composer had a hissy fit about the premiere being in provincial Wells rather than London. Disappointingly diva, if true.

In any case, he would have been upstaged by Louis, a large ginger cat and Wells cathedral legend who was keen to guest with the orchestra. Evidently unmoved by the modern stuff, Louis only put in an appearance for the Tchaikovsky, taking up his position to the right of the orchestra, curled up among the cellos. Only when a pretty young oboist carried him off was the performance able to proceed. While the orchestra tuned up, Louis found a vacant seat, behind me, where he purred contentedly for half an hour or so until he too fell asleep.

After a brief and exuberant encore of the music to The Magnificent Seven (the number of sober musicians in the orchestra?) that woke Louis, we were on our way back to Kent, a four hour journey broken thankfully briefly at Fleet services. One o'clock in the morning, in a smelly service station cafe, deserted except for tired truckers and bleary-eyed and dishevelled holidaymakers, with what was unequivocally the worst espresso I have ever been offered with a straight face.

The music on the Tannoy was Back to black. By Amy Winehouse.

August

I don't know what's going on in the world sometimes. I open a newspaper to the sight of global financial meltdown. Graphs of share prices in freefall, pictures of anxious traders tugging their hair out, grim and apocalyptic predictions of recession or depression. Parallels being drawn with the 1929 crash or Black Wednesday (was it a Wednesday -- I forget).

Talk is of a double dip recession. And despite the alluring reference to ice cream toppings, double dip is not a good thing. America's credit rating is questioned and the whole world is drawn into a vortex of financial insecurity.

Thanks Uncle Sam -- I loved the hamburgers, jeans and the 1959 Cadillac Eldorado. I was even prepared to put up with endless reruns of Friends. But enough is enough guys!

I switch on the television for some respite. There is none. While the world's markets collapse, Britain's cities burn. On every channel, there are burning cars, shops being looted and residents terrified. Its Beirut, Tripoli and Baghdad all rolled into one. What is going on?

CRAYFISH
Friday 5th August 2011

When an airline's principal marketing tagline is "the on-time airline" it is apparent that the bar is not being set very high. No mention of excellent service, delicious food, or extensive routes. No. We will get you there roughly on time, that's it. Oh, and bring your own sarnies. I half expected them to charge for using the toilet. And the seats were about as far apart as electron orbitals. Pigs in farrowing crates fare better. This is the air travel experience stripped to the bare bones. In fact not so much stripped down to the bare bones as picked clean by vultures. Short of abandoning maintenance or charging passengers for breathing, it's hard to see where further economies could be made.

The same goes for the destination airport. We flew into 'Stockholm Vasteras" airport, yet another of BrianAir's airport destinations that is a day's travel from the nominal city (Vasteras is 102km to the northwest of Stockholm, as far as Brighton is from London). At least it was not busy. As far as I could see, one international flight per day. We were met by Agnetha with a "tractor" she had hired for us on the erroneous assumption that a car the size of an armoured personnel carrier can be successfully powered by a tiny diesel engine generating as much power as a domestic lightbulb. Still, it did go. Sort of.

Agnetha and Loki had invited us to join them for several days at their summer house on the lakes near Engelsberg. The house, hidden away in the forest, is accessible only on foot. We abandoned the tractor and dragged our bags through the woods on a hand-drawn trailer. In a glade, set back from the water, was a tiny hamlet of related houses. Near the main dwelling were the "lighthouse", the "brown house" and wood stores. Down the slope to the jetty was a beach house, silent but for the gentle lapping of waves on the rocks of the lake shore. Nearby was a barrel-shaped sauna.

We stayed for five timeless days, soaking up the calm of this special place. No teleconferences, no deadlines, no reports and reviews. Just fishing, swimming, eating and drinking. And when it comes to eating and drinking, midsummer in Sweden is the place to be – a time when Swedes rediscover their viking roots. I half expected to see longships on the lake.

Midsummer in particular is a huge celebration in Sweden. Although we were a few weeks late for the actual day of the festival, we were given a pretty thorough reincarnation of it, sitting outside with a cauldron of lake crayfish and enthusiastic singing (if that's the word) fuelled by aquavit. Home-made aquavit is something of a tradition here, with competitions for the most unusual flavourings. Some work, some don't. Wormwood and coriander is a combo that, if I'm brutally honest, falls in the latter category. In the same way that potassium cyanide and strawberry might. Or arsenic and elderflower. I can still taste it a week later.

The songs, led by Tor and Petra, old friends of Loki began simply enough with ditties about student drinking. As the aquavit took hold they became increasingly slurred and our hosts increasingly hesitant of providing English translations while the children were within earshot. It didn't matter - while we ate and drank until belts creaked under the tension, their children shrieked and giggled in the forest like woodland sprites.

Loki likes crayfish. Actually nobody likes crayfish more than Loki. I ate maybe ten. By the time the sun headed gently to the horizon, barely skimming the clouds, Loki finally closed the book on the crayfish with a personal tally around thirty, sitting contentedly among a pile of shells in a haze of beer and schnapps.

And then, as if we weren't already sated, we took chairs and a blueberry crumble down to the jetty where we started on the Swedish punch, a drink composed of sugar, herbs and aviation fuel as far as I can tell. Loki and Agnetha kept a supply under the house in the kind of bottles associated more with lab chemicals than your local off-licence. The orange Hazchem symbol seemed strangely appropriate. "You will hate it" said Agnetha, pouring me a glass.

Strange, but I don't remember the sun setting that night.

DISCIPLINE
Tuesday 9th August 2011

Well I have to say that I'm jolly unimpressed with this civil disorder malarkey. I come back from a lovely restful holiday in Sweden to find my own country going to the dogs. A fortnight ago, we had nothing more weighty to worry about than remembering to pack suntan lotion. A week later, and we return to a bad day in Soweto. The country's youth appear to be setting fire to cars and pelting the police with missiles whilst helping themselves to armfuls of electrical goods more or less around the clock. "How do you wish to pay sir? Molotov cocktail - that'll do nicely". Looting in Tooting, stealing in Ealing, riotous assembly in Wembley. Well, call me old-fashioned but I don't think that's on. Bring back birching, I hear my grandmother say.

At primary school, I had a teacher -- a strong disciplinarian in the Enoch Powell mould and a product of the Colonial service -- who would carry a cane with him and administer roadside justice as he saw fit. To him all adolescent boys were criminals. If not criminals already, then latent villains merely waiting for the opportunity to turn bad. Mr Tonks saw no good in anyone. All apparent acts of kindness made him suspicious. The mere act of saying thank you to him was enough to set his eye twitching. He wore an ill fitting monocle which, when his eye twitched, would plop into his tea. If his target was out of range of the cane, he would hurl the board rubber at the miscreant with surprising accuracy, filling the air with clouds of chalk.

In afternoon lessons, he would set us long pieces of Latin comprehension while he read the Telegraph or snoozed. Sometimes we would wake him at the end of the lesson. Sometimes not, as he would wake with all the charm of a startled wildebeest and, as often as not, reach for the cane. I remember the hubbub when 4A had reached the end of double Latin and a particularly testing piece of Virgil and, unable to rouse Mr Tonks ffrom slumber, had alerted the staffroom. Mr Hay, the headmaster, practically ran. But to no avail. Mr Tonks was already cold, having died an hour earlier, halfway through the Telegraph crossword. 14 Down: author of the Aeneid (6).

So tricky was the Latin translation, that nobody had noticed him slumped forward. Tim Bates, more than once the recipient of Mr Tonks's cane, saw this as divine retribution and said it just went to prove that Latin was a dead language.

Mr Tonks would have had no truck with civil misbehaviour. As someone who would happily cane pupils for talking in class, one can hardly imagine the justice he would have meted out for looting. I still remember the occasion when 3B asked him to talk about his Second World War experiences in morning assembly. You could have cut the tension with a knife. But then most of us had never seen a grenade before.

You could have heard a pin drop.

EYELASHES AND MORE
Sunday 14th August 2011

Holidays. Is there anything more stressful than going on a family holiday?

Friday. Claire has left detailed instructions - she is working on Friday so I am charged with masterminding the packing. In best managerial style, I delegate the task - I think 'empowered' was the word I used - to each of my offspring. Each is to take responsibility for their own packing. At five, I check progress.

"Alex, are you packed?"

"Yes" says Alex in a voice that years of experience have taught me means the opposite.

"What have you packed?"

"A hoodie and a pair of sandals".

Leaving aside the fact that this is not much to show for the last two hours, I remind him we will be away for two weeks. He is unabashed. Evidently he plans to loot anything else he might need. But this 'laissez faire' attitude will not wash with his mother so I suggest he might like to revisit the concept of holiday packing before Claire returns from work and chooses his clothes for him. If he wants to look like a New York rapper, he will have to do it himself. If he wants to look like Rupert Bear, no action is needed on his part.

The thought that his mother might actually pick his holiday wardrobe has an immediate salutary effect and he resumes the task with the kind of focus seldom mustered for say homework, passing Alice on the stairs.

Alice is struggling downstairs with a suitcase the size of a family hatchback. I ask her if she has packed for two weeks or is starting a new life in some remote part of Asia. People emigrate with less. Only when she opens the suitcase, under protest it should be noted, does Alice's idea of packing become clear. Apart from a pair of Dolce and Gabbana sunglasses and a pink bikini the size of a Rizla, the rest seems to be entirely cosmetics. "They're all essential, before you say anything" says Alice. I count to ten before suggesting, with my usual egregious tact and diplomacy, that she only has to paint one face, not the Sistine Chapel roof. The look I receive from Alice tells me instantly that this will not be one of those cherished father-daughter bonding moments. In fact there may not be any more of them. Ever. I invite her to lose a few kilos of cosmetics, in the knowledge that she will not meet anyone she knows in Brittany. Blusher breakup, mascara meltdown or lackadaisical lipstick application will go unreported.

An hour later and Alex looks like Ali G. Alice looks like thunder. Neither are in holiday mood. Nor ready for the two hour drive to Portsmouth, my cunning plan to avoid pre-holiday stress. We have to catch an early morning ferry from Portsmouth to Caen. So rather than wake the family in dead of night and echo my parents' wild races against the clock, I book us into a Portsmouth hotel the night before the ferry. No dishevelled quayside arrivals. We would wake refreshed with only a short schlepp to the port. Simple.

We are barely twenty miles of bickering along the road when Alice says we have to turn round. She has forgotten her eyelash curlers. I make it clear that my analysis of the situation has led me to a different conclusion and one that, as driver, I intend to implement. We drive on in silence.

Around   ten   o'clock   we   pull   in   to   the PremierTravelWesternMetro Hotel, tired and dishevelled. At this late hour, our dining options are more or less limited to the Tubby Carvery next door. Being, as I mentioned, ten o'clock on a Friday night in a naval town, this is a rather - how shall I say - robust dining environment. The pub quiz is drawing to a close in a flurry of smutty jokes and we are asked to hurry to the carvery before 'chef' calls it a day. On the evidence of the food, 'chef' had run out of inspiration and called it a day sometime in the mid 1960s. I didn't think places like this still existed. Against our better judgement, and to a chorus of cackling from a hen party at table 15, we eat a quantity of meat more commonly associated with a lion kill on the plains of the Serengeti. The prospect of 'mouthwatering Black Forest gateau' to follow feels more like a threat than a promise and I sheepishly ask for the bill.

By the time the alarm clock rings, all hope of sleep has been abandoned. Indigestion has
inevitably meant a night of unsettlingly vivid dreams. Such as being chased around the carvery by some mythical beast - half great white shark, half Black Forest gateau. With tentacles. And a hat marked 'chef'.

Alice glares at me from beneath uncurled lashes. She reserves the right to go vegetarian again and it's all my fault.

SAMEDI EN FRANCE
Wednesday 17th August 2011

Saturday morning. Having begun so inauspiciously at the Tubby Carvery in Portsmouth, the holiday picks up once we are on board the Normandie. Although some twenty years old, the ship feels fresh, modern and well equipped, Alice can buy cosmetics in the Duty Free and, best of all, the onboard catering is done by the French. Fresh brioche or stale toast? Your call. The food even sounds better in French. Who could possibly want the depressingly laconic "burger and chips" when you could have the poetry of "steak hache et pommes allumettes"? I rest my case.

As we head out past Gosport and one of those menacing old Napoleonic defence towers that scatter the south coast, the gentle sway of the ship - it's actually blowing a fair breeze - turns everyone aboard into Parkies as they struggle to get their sea legs. It's nice to let them into my world for a moment or two. Let's see how you manage, I think to myself. Kids are the worst, bouncing off tables like some human pinball machine. Bumped heads abound.

Once past the Isle of Wight and into the sea lanes, the water is surprisingly calmer, the breeze now mollified to a gentle zephyr. Just as well. The channel is full of shipping in August. Giant container ships and tankers jostle cheek by jowl with yachts and pleasure craft in a slow ballet. We weave between them until a rising drone from the diesels signals clear water and we make for Caen.

I settle down with Mike Brearley's staggeringly insightful 'The Art of Captaincy', determined to implement its findings in my last game for the club on my return from France. A tad late in my cricketing career, I grant you, but who cares. Claire and Alice are having girly shopping time while Alex is learning the rules of poker, presumably with a view to supplementing his holiday money at the expense of any local French children.

The journey passes quickly and, before we know, the French coast looms and we are disembarking in grey rain at Ouisterham. Nonchalant shrugs from the Douanes and we are on the autoroute to Dol de Bretagne. To you and I, an autoroute is just a motorway. But to young Michel in his rusty Peugeot and mirrored Raybans, it is evidently a qualifier for Le Mans 2012. He closes to within a few inches of our bumper, so close I can see the whites of his eyes. To save all our lives, I move over and catch a definite whiff of Gauloises as he snarls past us at ninety. Probably to the sound of accordion music. The D roads are better, more deserted. But even here, you can drive as little as a mile before the rear view mirror is filled by an overrevving 2CV apparently intent on joining the suitcase in the boot.

We have learned through bitter experience that there are no shops open on Sundays in France. And few cafes or restaurants. This can catch out the unwary English traveller. Spending the sabbath as a day of fasting and abstinence may be a good way of preparing for a pilgrimage or a day of devotions. It is, I can assure you, much less spiritually cleansing when it forms an unexpected part a family holiday. Although we have been assured Sunday shopping is better in August, we take no chances and stop by the Carrefour for a few staples - wine, bread, milk, saucisson, wine, cheese, fruit and wine. Oh and wine.

Through Dol de Bretagne, then a few miles south on the road to Combourg and we pull in to a swishy gravel drive. I have barely switched off the engine before we are greeted with a pulverisingly good gin and tonic by David and Ginny, owners of the gite. We talk cricket - England have just won the third test - while Jack and Mollie, their two young chocolate labradors, sniff and nose us for treats, quickly losing interest when we have none.

We uncork a bottle of Saumur-Champigny, slice saucisson and cheese into baguettes, and watch the sunset to a chorus of cicadas. Does it get any better?

GRIDIRON
Saturday 20th August 2011

In the early 1980s, my kid brother Charlie and I shared a flat. And our Sunday evenings from September to January each year followed a fixed pattern - popcorn, lager and the radio tuned to the Armed Forces Network. Because on Sunday night, the AFN broadcast American Football. Gridiron. The NFL.

Channel 4 had introduced the UK to the fast pace and razzamatazz of American Football in 1980 although, like most in the UK, we could not understand how a game could call itself football when the foot was more or less the only part of the body that didn't touch the ball. Unless you were a specialist kicker or punter, you used your hands. And only your hands. You threw, caught or ran with the ball. It came as no surprise then that, to score a touchdown, the one thing you were not required to do was actually touch the ball down.

But this football taught us a new language - where pockets were not in trousers but in that evanescent fluid space between centre, guards and tackles, where sacks were not bags but tallies of defensive mayhem wreaked by ends and nose tackles and where turnovers were not made of pastry and contained no apple.

It was a game where half backs and tight ends created tiny gaps for a full back to blast through. A game where a completion was often a beginning rather than an end. A game where safeties, free or strong, forced fumbles and cornerbacks leapt for interceptions. And a game where quarterbacks pumped, faked, passed or scrambled while linebackers blitzed. It was a game of offence and defence, pronounced Off-ence and Dee-fence.

And the more one watched the game, the more a pattern emerged from chaos, the more one saw the shape and structure of the game. What looked at first like 22 men pushing and jostling each other, like a scene from a Gateshead nightclub, soon resolved itself into an explosive drama of interweaving patterns, lines and movements. It may not have been chess but there was structure. Fleet-footed receivers glided round the distant periphery while knuckle-scraping Neanderthals bludgeoned each other into submission in the middle and linebackers, like slavering dogs, barked and snarled in the quarterback's face.

But, like so many in the UK, we were seduced not by the chalkboard patterns but by the bright colours, fast action, drama and excitement of gridiron. Not to mention the cheerleaders. You certainly didn't see anything like that at the Doncaster Rovers - Barnsley game. But for Charlie and I, the weekly Channel 4 TV broadcast barely whetted our appetite. We couldn't wait a week - we wanted to know the scores as they came in, touchdown by touchdown.

These of course were pre-internet days. Finding out the scores in 1980 meant the crackle and fadeouts of short wave radio. It was like stepping back in time. You could imagine snowbound Wisconsin prairie farmers huddled round the radio in the 1950s as the Packers slugged it out with the Vikings in a Green Bay blizzard. Or 70s barbecue parties in Miami and Tampa yelping and whooping as the Dolphins and Buccaneers traded touchdowns in the September sunshine. For years, fading in and out amid the crackle and hiss we would hear excited shrieks of "Touchdown", "Fumble" and "Turnover".

"The Bears are showing blitz... the ball is snapped...Marino on a three step drop... has Duper in double coverage..... he's going to have to hurry... Marino pumps .... Clayton is open... he throws.... caught and out of bounds at the 24".

But more than the game itself, Channel 4 and the AFN also introduced us to a new set of sporting heroes - quarterback Dan Marino, running back Walter Payton, wide receiver Steve Largent, and safety Ronnie Lott were the big stars at that time. But none of these was bigger than William 'The Refrigerator' Perry. When the Bears were within a yard of the opposition goal line, they would hand the ball to The Fridge. Tipping the scales at over 310 pounds, Perry would never win a sprint but over a couple of yards he was as unstoppable as a runaway freight train. He would clutch the ball to his chest and rumble over the goal line trampling opposition linebackers into the mud.

And as with real football - or soccer as my American friends insist on misnaming it - Charlie and I supported different teams. Charlie's allegiances lay with the brutal Raiders, the bad boys of the NFL, with their stars Marcus Allen, Lester Hayes, Howie Long and Jim Plunkett.

But for me, the real poetry in the game came from across the bay where San Francisco Fortyniner quarterback Joe Montana and his receivers Jerry Rice and Dwight Clark picked opposition defences apart in a magnificent, choreographed aerial ballet. And when Montana retired, Steve Young seamlessly assumed the mantle, as Owens later did for Rice. And these were halcyon days for the Fortyniners. Five trips to the Superbowl and five victories.

Times move on - the internet allows one to monitor fifteen games, ball by ball in a haze of on-screen stats. More information than Charlie or I could possibly have needed. but somehow it's not the same. The sterility of the internet cannot match the passion of live commentary and craning to hear the commentator's words amid the static.

"Montana to Rice....Touchdown Fortyniners!"

FLORA
Tuesday 23rd August 2011

Flora, our beloved dog, died unexpectedly last week, on the 16th August. We were on holiday in France when the kennels called to say she had been taken ill. The vets who had operated on her painted a grim picture and prepared us for the worst. The call the following morning was brief but sympathetic. Flora was gone. I took a few minutes before calling back. We discussed arrangements briskly in a matter of fact way. Just a dog, after all.

But anyone who has ever owned one will know that a dog is more than just a dog. Try telling Catherine, who was 10 years old, that the whimpering puppy she comforted all the way home from the breeder's was 'just a dog'. Try telling Alex, the small boy who would sleep curled up on the floor beside her that Flora was 'just a dog'. Try telling Alice, who would dress her up in hats and scarves, that Flora was 'just a dog'.

Flora was 'just a dog' in the sense that a Rolls Royce is 'just a car'.

Flora, or Pannacotta Bellissima Floribunda in her full majesty, joined our family in 2002. One of only two whites in a litter of otherwise black standard poodles, she was the beauty - the belle - of the litter. She was the one the breeder wanted to keep, the one whose departure left her sobbing. A special dog.

And how right she was. From the moment she joined us, Flora enriched our lives in ways beyond the scope of the word to express. Some dogs will always be dogs, their occasional barks, growls or snaps a periodic reminder of their identity and that we enter the canine world on their terms. But Flora was human. She preferred the company of people to that of dogs. And she preferred her humans to others. She adapted herself to our ways, not us to hers. She idolised us. We were her sun, moon and stars.

Some dogs are 'good with children'. Flora was brilliant. She could be pushed and pulled, poked and prodded. Never once did she growl or express intolerance at her human family. If you were happy or sad, Flora was there. If you wanted a listener, Flora was there, gently nuzzling you or resting her head on your lap, gazing at you though liquid brown eyes. No matter how bad your day had been, Flora would make it better.

A saint of a dog.

Dusty theologians, with hawkish heads and empty hearts, tell us dogs have no soul, and that there will be none in heaven. Robert Louis Stevenson didn't buy that any more than I do. "You think dogs will not be in heaven? I tell you, they will be there long before any of us" he said. If there is a heaven, there will assuredly be dogs in it. How could it be heaven otherwise?

And Flora will be there, waiting faithfully by the gate, till that day when we walk again together. Why else would there be a patron saint for dogs?

He is Saint Roch and his feast day is the 16th August.

MARKET DAY
Saturday 27th August 2011

It's Lundi. Monday. Market day in Combourg. Despite high excitement the previous evening over the prospect, I am, as usual, the only one awake. My insomnia has scaled new heights this holiday. A moth fluttering its wings in the Southern Pacific could wake me. The moment Thierry the farmer coaxes his spluttering 2CV into life, I am awake. It's cinq heures. And dark still. By neuf heures, I am still the only one awake. The rest of the Rip van Winkle family do not stir.

While the house sleeps I have been on my usual nightly visit to Club Insomnia, written two thousand words of descriptive prose and, through the privacy of headphones, heard the world end. As the last chords of Götterdämmerung ring out, the Rhine overflows and Valhalla burns. Alex stumbles, bleary-eyed, downstairs and immediately plugs in his iPod.

"Hey dad" he murmurs "wassup?".

"The world has ended"

"Bummer" he shrugs

"Well quite"

Alex opens the fridge. Last night's imaginatively improvised cassoulet or a family-size bag of mixed fruit Carambar chews. From somewhere he finds a half empty bottle of Orangina. Alice glides down the stairs, sags onto the sofa and jabs the remote at the TV. 'There's nothing on" she announces after two or three petulant button presses.

"Can I interest you in the end of the world?" I venture, offering her the headphones.

"Nah. Wagner's boring" says Alice, crushingly dismissing the Master's entire oeuvre in three words.

I remind them it is market day. Despite the excitement shown yesterday at the prospect of wall-to-wall patisserie, the children are now in no particular hurry to strip Combourg of its pain chocolats. But the management, in the form of Claire, wants sticky cakes and will not be thwarted. She chivvies the kids along, suggesting that their cooperation in this matter will be rewarded by crepes and the kind of sugar buzz more commonly associated with Class A drugs. Alex, immune to desserts, is unmoved but trades his acquiescence for pizza.

The girls buy pretty scarves and some sort of kit of potions for painting floral motifs on their nails. Alex wants a tomtom from a stall run by the darkest Senegalese negro I have ever seen. I buy two studded leather biker belts, both extraordinary value, but also the wrong size, a fact only apparent when home. My daughters tut-tut. A rookie error. "Have you taken your medication?" they ask, as though this might explain the financial and sartorial lapse. "Lots" I reply with a wink.

An hour later and we are lurching back to the car, weighed down by melons, saucissons, cheeses, artichokes, farmhouse cider and the near legendary Kouign Amann. For those unfamiliar with Breton cookery, the Kouign Amann takes some explaining. It contains only flour, sugar, egg and butter but, like a souffle, is so much more than the sum of its parts. The recipe, although closely guarded, consists fundamentally of two steps (I'm not giving much away here).

1.   Fold as much butter into a sugar, egg and flour mixture as it can possibly hold.
2.   Then add a lot more.

Catherine describes it as 'extreme croissant'. We buy one the size of a landmine in an earthenware dish. Only when we are left with a surprisingly light dish at the end of the meal do we realise how much of the weight had been the Kouign Amann. And how much of that had been butter. We think better of any undue postprandial exertion in the swimming pool.

David, the gite owner, beckons me over, as he has done several times already this holiday. We are both wine lovers with a taste for the unusual. "I guarantee you won't have tasted this before" he says, with a conspiratorial twinkle in his eye, and pours me a glass. It is a deep ruby and has a striking cherry and spice nose. I am puzzled. Too spicy for Pinot Noir? Wrong fruit for Syrah, surely. Could it even be a vin d'etranger? I just about guess its age right. David's clue that it is a burgundy leaves me floundering because this is not a typical example. Much chin rubbing on my part before, with a flourish, David shows me the label. It is a red Meursault. Yes, red. As rare as hen's teeth. I wouldn't have got it in a month of Sundays.

"Never mind" says Alice "It's not the end of the world".

ROYAL FLUSH
Tuesday 30th August 2011

This is worrying. Over the course of our holiday, Alex has developed quite a taste for cards. If it were whist or bridge, this might be excusable. Social games. Games that encourage conviviality and stimulate conversation. A hand or two of gin rummy perhaps or canasta maybe? These would all be acceptable cardplaying. Games that his parents might even endorse as a means of teaching an adolescent boy social skills and graces.

But no. Alex has turned to the dark side of cardplaying. Not for him the idle chitchat of whist. Nor the social niceties of bridge. No sirree. Alex wants to play poker. A game for monosyllabic sociopaths driven by the desire to humiliate opponents. When did you last hear anyone concede a hand with "Well played, old chap"? Or indeed any form of compliment?

Bridge conveys afternoon images of maiden aunts in floral print dresses, tea from bone china cups and almond macaroons. Poker means Uncle Leroy and his buddies, awash with beer, whisky and crisps, shouting and swearing long into the night. While bridge is a game of refinement, there is something vaguely feral about poker. If bridge was a pedigree Siamese cat, poker would be an unneutered polecat.

I am personally wary too of any card game associated with gambling. Being, on a daily basis, pumped full of dopamine agonists, I am doubly cautious. Gambling is one of the most widely acknowledged problems associated with the use of dopamine agonists in Parkinson's. And it's not surprising really. These drugs act on the brain's reward centres, increasing our desire to take risks. Overtaking on blind bends, bungee jumping, that sort of thing. And, of course, gambling. It doesn't happen to everyone. It doesn't even happen to most. But it does happen to some and, for those affected, it can be cataclysmic, swiftly eating into savings. "So it's like a drug" says Alice, somehow grasping and not grasping at the same time.

Maybe I've been lucky, if that's what I mean, but I've never had the desire to gamble. I have bought only one lottery ticket in my entire life, and that only to please my younger daughter who, following two earlier misfortunes that day, felt certain that luck must therefore favour her. Third time lucky? Needless to say, the death of her guinea pig and (temporary) loss of her mobile phone proved to be poor predictors of the outcome of El Gordo that evening.

As a scientist I've always espoused the rather smug view that the lottery is little more than a tax on people who are bad at maths. If that appears holier than thou, it perhaps belies my own concerns over gambling. These things tend to run in families and my grandfather, enthusiastic patron of the Black Bull, was equally fond of the cards. So being cautious, perhaps overcautious, that one royal flush will send me on a downward spiral to destitution, I tend to avoid all card games.

There is a certain irony to this. Our blank expressionless faces, that so distress our loved ones, are almost ideal for poker. Whether I am holding a full house or a pair of twos, my face remains resolutely immobile. The ultimate poker face. My grandfather would have killed for it. Which is more than can be said for my tremor which increases in direct proportion to the hand held. A low pair and I have the steady hands of a concert pianist. Four kings and my arm becomes a flapping seal fin.

Despite my reservations, I tend to join in the evening poker session. We play strictly for counters despite Alex's several covert attempts to establish a counter-to-Euro exchange rate. Where's the harm, I ask myself. A bit of family fun.

Alex, increasingly acquiring the card shuffling skills of a croupier, deals while Alice, affecting an air of casual disinterest, thumbs through French Vogue between hands. Claire and I are merely there as cannon fodder. Inevitably, the games follow a standard pattern, with me quickly bankrupted by my barometric tremor. Actually I tend to be the second out, after Claire who has no concept of the rules and persistently asks questions like "Are spades worth the same as hearts?" or "Does it matter if I've got all the aces?" Alex puts his head in his hands. Claire and I return to the Times crossword and a glass or two of Saussignac. "Play nicely" we say.

An hour later it's all gone quiet. Ominously quiet so I poke my head discreetly round the door. Both are engrossed. And the counters are nowhere to be seen. Alice has her back to me.

"I see your Raybans and raise you an iPod" she says.

September

You took away my tears...

        ...but gave me reasons to cry

You took away my appetite...

        ...but gave me a new hunger for life

You took my independence...

        ...but gave me friends to rely on

You took away my sleep...

        ...but filled my head with dreams

You took away my speech...

        ...but gave me a voice

You took away the light...

        ...but gave me a torch in the darkness

You took away my future...

        ...but gave me back my present

When there is nothing left to take...

        ...we have everything to give

Taken from 'Give and Take', a video project collaboration on individual attitudes to the adjustments needed when living with Parkinson's

(c) Sara Riggare & Jon Stamford 2011

FRANGLAIS
Saturday 4th September 2011

It's bad enough that the French have utter contempt for British cooking. But I sometimes feel that our stumbling British efforts to order the fruits of French cuisine are met with equal derision.

It's early in our holiday and I have managed to fill the car with diesel (gazole) without mechanistic mishap. The car is still running and I am on a linguistic roll. I have spent hours immersed in the French phrase book and my best 'plume de ma tante' schoolboy French is flooding back to me. I announce to the children that "we will eat out tonight". Alice and Alex exchange nervous glances. We have been here before and the prospect of their father yet again making a public spectacle of himself - and, let's face it, them - with overconfident linguistic exploits fills them with horror. Like watching their father dance, the embarrassment potential is limitless. At least their father no longer dances outside the house.

So we arrive at the Hotel des Sables in our holiday clothes. As we enter the dining room, heads turn and the murmur of conversation quietens a little. We are, by a couple of decades, the youngest people there. We are also the only diners in shorts. We look like Martians. The head waiter's nostrils flare. He raises one Gallic eyebrow.

"Monsieur?"

"Quatre couverts s'il vous plait" I reply in my best Baedeker French.

In those few words I have dashed the waiter's hopes that we might simply be lost travellers seeking directions. We plan to eat. There is a moment's pause before he leads us to a table in the middle of the room. Evidently we are to be put on display. He leaves four menus and walks away, weaving between tables and exchanging words with the other diners. The only word I catch is 'Anglais', greeted at each table by knowing looks and barely suppressed laughter.

A minute or so later, and before I have fully translated the menu for the kids, Gaston returns. "Vous avez choisi?" he asks in a theatrically loud voice. Around the room, I am aware of other diners turning to watch the spectacle. I quickly pick the 'menu a seize Euros' and confidently read our choices from the parade of 'fruits de mer, volailles, assiette Breton' and so forth on offer.

"Pardon monsieur". With a shrug Gaston the garcon feigns incomprehension "Le saumon, oui? Mais en quel facon?" There are titters. He knows perfectly well that the salmon is served 'en croute' so I am at a loss to explain the cabaret. I soldier on. We are clearly not going to be friends. No Christmas card from him.

"Er... je veux... pardon... je voudrais... la... le?... salade de poule...er...poulet (I make discreet flapping movements)...s'il vous plait." Always remember to say please, if nothing else, I remind myself. Somehow, even with the ever helpful waiter on hand to point out my linguistic shortcomings, we manage to order our food. Being Brittany we have plumped for fish or white meat. Safe choices nutritionally even in the French quicksands Gaston is determined to inflict upon his sartorially inadequate charges.

"Et comme boisson?" he asks, largely to the wider room. The English traditionally know nothing about wine and the wine list is therefore a potential minefield. There is a palpable hush of anticipation around the room as the waiter, like a cat playing with a mouse, goes for the kill.

But, even if the language is not, the 'Carte des Vins' is very much my territory. I flick through with a feigned air of disinterest before closing the wine list with a dismissive flourish. "Le Chablis Vaillons 2008, s'il vous plait". An austere but noble white wine from a strong vintage. A wine that will complement our food perfectly. More to the point, a wine that tells the waiter that I know my stuff. Even if I dress like a beach bum. There is a murmur of respect from the other diners.

Gaston nods. He has been beaten on his own turf. He says nothing to the other tables as he slinks away. I wait until he has gone a few yards before I call out to him "et aussi de Badoit". He pauses momentarily before nodding in acknowledgement. If the wine alone had not won the battle, the choice of water merely rubbed it in. Badoit is the foodie's choice but, more than that, an indicator of knowledge.

The waiter knows I have won. But, better still, he knows that I know he knows I have won.

PIE AND A PINT
Friday 9th September 2011

I don't know about you, but to me there are few pleasures more intense than sitting in a comfortable armchair by a crackling log fire in The Elephant's Head, The Spotted Dog or The Hare -- or any number of attractive watering holes dotted around the Kent-Sussex border. As you open the door, the smell of burning apple wood greets you like incense. A decent pint of bitter and a slice of game pie and all is well with the world.

Strangely, although a Yorkshireman by lineage, I acquired my taste for real ale during many years in the West Country -- first Wiltshire and later Somerset (there was no Avon in those days, except as a river). And when it came to beer, Wiltshire meant the Wadworth Brewery in Devizes and their most estimable product, 6X.

Now many of you think you know 6X, the distinctive blue and white cans on supermarket shelves. And, enjoyable though that drink indubitably is, it bears little semblance to the 6X of my youthful memory, the sweetish malty nectar pulled by hand pump from deep cellars or -- best of all -- drawn directly from a barrel behind the bar. Wadworths did not can their beer in those days. If you wanted a pint of 6X, you had to be in Wiltshire at the very least. If you wanted to be sure of tasting the beer in its prime, a pilgrimage to Devizes was obligatory.

In the late seventies Devizes had thirty two pubs, ranging from the hideous (Formica-bedecked , strip light illuminated transport cafes) to the cosy (canalside pubs with saggy leather armchairs, inglenook fireplaces and blackened beams). Of those thirty two pubs, twenty eight were Wadworths tied houses. Heaven.

Well, I say heaven but that's the fifty three-year-old Jon speaking. Knock off three and a half decades, and it was a very different Jon in search of his pint. A Jon who would happily stand for hours in a crowded pub, pint in hand, engrossed in conversation with his friends and oblivious -- or at the very least disinterested -- in his surroundings. Wipe down Wimpy bar Formica went unnoticed. Even piped music, normally enough to make me foam at the mouth, would not dampen my ardour for the ale. I would even tolerate jukeboxes. The Jon of today, old Parkypants himself, would put up with none of this. And incidentally who invented the brim pint – I defy you to find me a single tremor-dominant Parkie who can get from bar to table without spilling it over the carpet or himself.

Whilst I was at university I saw fit to dedicate many long evenings to the production of the ultimate guide to Bath pubs. This work, sadly languishing unpublished in an upstairs drawer, was to be the definitive assessment of the city's many hostelries. The book would be to Bath pubs what Wisden has been to cricket. Working on the theory that there were some four thousand students at Bath and that, of those, one could conservatively say that perhaps ninety nine percent were interested in fermentation products of one form or another, I developed a simple business model -- If each of these paid the very reasonable sum of say fifty pence for a copy of my Bath pub guide, that would amount to a purse slightly short of two thousand pounds. Or put another way, a year's student grant (this was 1979 remember).

Such a substantial sum placed certain responsibilities on the shoulders of the author and necessitated a commensurate effort on behalf of the writer to match the anticipated income stream. To produce this magnum opus, a phenomenal amount of on-site research was needed. No stone was left unturned, no beer undrunk. Landlords were quizzed in penetrating detail about their beer, its storage and any other features of the pub that would enhance one's beer drinking experience. Nothing was left to chance in what was to be a work of supreme scholarship. In the same way that Jesus turned water into wine, I planned to turn a student grant into best bitter.

In the end, pubs were graded on a 0 to 100 scale although some pubs somehow achieved more than 100 points. And I adopted a simple, if highly personal and prejudiced, marking scheme. Each pub would start with 50 points, with additional points being added or removed accordingly. Let me give you a flavour:

- No real ales: -20 points
- More than two real ales: +20 points
- More than two real ales of which one was Wadworths 6X: +50 points

- Range of bar snacks including at least two of pork scratchings, Bombay mix, Quavers or Monster Munch: +20 points
- Nothing but peanuts and ready salted crisps: -20 points

- Friendly landlord: +10 points
- Unfriendly or difficult landlord: -10 points
- Unfriendly or difficult landlord but with surprisingly fetching barmaid daughter: +20 points

- Home-made food: +30 points
- Adding a sprig of parsley to a supermarket Cornish pasty and calling it home-made: -30 points

- Dog: +5 points as long as it makes no effort to steal your pork scratchings

- Yapping dog: -30 points
- Yapping dog with amorous intentions towards one's leg: -50 points or, subject to absence of fetching barmaid at the premises, possible disqualification from the guide.

- Blonde barmaid: +20 points for each up to a maximum of five
- Blonde barmaid prepared to give you her phone number: +50 points

As you've probably gathered, this was a work of, at best, dubious scholarship. What began with unquestionable methodological integrity had somehow slipped a few rungs down the ethical ladder. Somehow, and this may come as no surprise to those of you with teenage sons, I had found myself drawing other extracurricular aspects of the pub into my appraisal of its merits. Understandable really and probably the reason why the book was never, probably could never be, published.

Come to think of it, I wonder whatever happened to Rosie from the Black Horse....

WHOLE BUNCH OF BIRTHDAYS
Wednesday 14th September 2011

In astronomical terms, it would be called a conjunction. One of those circumstances when the planets all align with each other and doomsayers predict huge city-engulfing tides, volcanic activity and pretty much anything short of a plague of frogs. Last weekend we had such an event. Claire, Alice and her cousin Peter have birthdays within a week of each other. For the most part this is a mere statistical anomaly, but on this particular occasion the birthdays concerned were a fiftieth and two eighteenths. Not birthdays that can be ignored.

So a few months ago, we decided to hold a large joint party. A party where we would invite all strands of the family.

Each of the birthday boys and girls was responsible for their own cake. Peter's cake had a photographic representation of the birthday boy himself beaming at the camera. Claire had chosen to pick out her age in yellow icing runny enough that each informative "50" looked dangerously like the rather confrontational "SO". A cake that invited you to step outside, whilst at the same time proving that there are limits to what you can achieve with detailed icing. But both of these paled into insignificance when set beside the towering edifice that was Alice's cake. If you can imagine the Bavarian castle of Neuschwanstein (that's the one in Chitty Chitty Bang Bang for the non-Wagnerians amongst you) entirely covered in fuchsia pink icing, you would not be far wrong. Ice cream cones and wafers formed turrets and battlements. If a cake was ever to require planning permission, this would be it.

Alone these would have been sufficient for the eighty or so guests who joined us. But driven by the maxim that nobody should go hungry, Alice had also baked Victoria sponges, coffee cakes, lemon drizzle takes and cupcakes in every colour and flavour. Two pasting tables, covered in white tablecloths, groaned under the weight of baking.

I had been vaguely aware that the kitchen was off-limits for a week or so before the party and that we were expected to fend for ourselves catering-wise -- there is incidentally, as I now know, a limit to how much pizza any family can reasonably be expected to endure -- but somehow even I was taken aback at the scale of the baking operation. Rather than attempt anything culinary, I took myself to the safe haven of the conservatory, ordered takeaway and opened a bottle of port.

On the whole my creative input into the party food discussion had been reduced to an advisory role, muttering from the sidelines, after my suggestion that loaves and fishes would be an appropriate catering solution for the numbers involved.

In an unexpected act of spouse empowerment, Claire asked me to resolve the question of drinks for the party. A task so simple that even I can be entrusted with it. I've long held the view that parties should be catered simply in terms of alcohol. If you provide booze for every eventuality, you will spend your entire afternoon mixing vodka martinis, Tom Collins, and things involving pink fluorescent spirits of with ridiculous names. Your guests will have long since departed before you realise you haven't had a chance to speak to any.

An hour later and I am in Majestic, probably my favourite place on earth, availing myself of their offer of the week -- Nicholas Feuillate champagne (2004 Vintage), a steal at £21 a bottle -- and a few other tempting little bijoux. In deference to the nondrinkers, I throw in a couple of cartons of orange juice and a bottle of Coke. Claire is aghast.

"Nearly half the guests are teetotal" she says.

"They won't be when they taste this champagne" I suggest "besides I bought orange juice".

Claire rolls her eyes skyward in one of those eloquent expressions of disappointment and I slink away to fetch more orange juice.

In the end it all passes off well. The garden looks magnificent, the marquees resplendent with balloons and ribbons. The weather is generous, warm zephyrs rather than autumn gales. And the guests come, from faraway corners of the country. But best of all, there are no speeches. Even Alice, tottering on six inch stiletto heels, manages to mingle among the throng without either breaking an ankle or spearing a relative's toes with her footwear.

"Is there any champagne?" asks Claire, kicking off her shoes after the last guests leave.

"All gone"

"Is there anything left to drink?"

"Yes" I replied "plenty of orange juice".

SHIPBUILDING PT 3: NOT FORGOTTEN
Monday 19th September 2011

Go on, be honest, you thought I had forgotten. You thought I had quietly shelved this project, choosing not to mention it further in tacit admission of defeat.

You should know me better by now. Okay the project has not proceeded at blistering pace but there is nonetheless progress. And it's progress on my terms. As I mentioned in a previous piece, I reserve the right to use cheats, shortcuts and fixes to achieve the end. I will rope in willing friends too. In other words the ship will become a metaphor for my life, a life in which I increasingly realise that I cannot do everything myself. It's a tough thing to ask someone to help at the best of times -- a grudging admission or acknowledgement of my failing body and its diminished powers – but I am learning to do so.

Thought you might be interested in a little history. The Danmark, a steel-hulled, double-bottomed, three-masted, full-rigger, was built at Nakskov Shipyard and is approximately 250 feet long. Danmark was launched in 1932 to train officers for the Danish Merchant Navy, but soon found favour with the civilian population too. The ship was modernised in 1959 and can be seen at her home port in Copenhagen.

So where have I got to? As with so much in life, nowhere near as far as I would like. The keel is down, and the vast majority of the hull is covered. Although this is a tiny fraction of the time that will be necessary, it is a high return sort of activity. Not a huge amount of work, but good bang for your buck. But that aside, why the slow progress? And it's not simply the Parkinson's. Or maybe it is but some more insidious facet of it. Not the shakes, stiffness or slowness of movement but some gentle sapping of will, some slow slide into apathy.

Or maybe in some way, it's a positive thing. I have a new job, and the job is stimulating and time-consuming. I enjoy the job and want to succeed. So maybe that means fewer hours spent on the Danmark.

Or perhaps it's just that summer means cricket. And organising cricket, making sure that teams are where they should be, that they have sandwiches and cake, and that they have all paid their match fees. So that takes care of the summer.

And when the nights draw in, my thoughts turn to genealogy -- to tracing ancestors back into the dark recesses of time. To forming that connection between past and present. It all takes time and, with Parkinson's, time is precious. Or maybe it's just a tacit admission that life gets in the way of planning and execution.

They say that people explain their actions in different ways. Am I avoiding the issue? Am I looking for reasons or for excuses? Do I want to complete the ship or am I looking for excuses not to? Procrastination is not generally part of Parkinson's. Often the reverse is true -- instead of putting off that trip of a lifetime, we bring it forward, mortgaging our futures with the collateral of our present.

A year ago, I went to hear a motivational speaker. No, don't get me wrong, this was a work commitment not an aberration of judgement. As most of you will be aware I am deeply suspicious of motivational speakers. I would put them on a par with homoeopathy. But still, there I was, forced to listen to a man who clearly regarded himself as the reincarnation of Jerry Lewis.

But in amongst the hours and hours of managerial newspeak and other mindsapping drivel, he did say one intelligent thing about motivation. He said that work was full of tasks we had to perform and those that one didn't and made the point that we derive little pleasure from tasks we are forced to do and the motivation came from being able to fit in the tasks we enjoy but don't have to do. In essence the icing on the cake. And he suggested that we focus on those aspects and by doing so, our day-to-day employment would be immeasurably richer.

It was a revelatory moment, which I guess was the intention. I concluded that, for me, the icing on the cake was nothing to do with work. I resigned the following Monday.

So which is the Danmark? Something I have to do or the icing on the cake? I honestly don't know. But as John Lennon said "life is what happens to you while you're busy making other plans".

THE DINNER PARTY
Friday 23rd September 2011

When I was young, my parents used to hold dinner parties. The auguries were easy to identify. We children would be sent upstairs for bed a good hour earlier than our normal bedtime. The gravity of the situation, a dinner party for the Doncaster academic glitterati, would be briefly outlined to us, along with the importance of us remaining upstairs at all costs. We were not to appear in the dining room demanding bedtime stories. Nor were we to amble downstairs requiring glasses of warm milk. Nor even seek assistance when Charlie got shampoo in his eyes. In fact we were not to appear in the dining room for any reason short of the impending destruction of the house. This was grown-up time and my parents did not wish to be interrupted. Sometimes our compliance would be bought with Jaffa cakes.

Invariably, when my brother and sister had fallen asleep, I would tiptoe downstairs and listen at the dining room door only to be disappointed by the conversation of the grown-ups who showed a dispiriting lack of meaningful conversation. Nothing about Action Man, steam trains, climbing frames or conkers. The local lawyers, surgeons and bankers clearly had nothing of interest to say.

Why couldn't my parents invite interesting people. Like the man in the bicycle clips who used to shout at the fruit in the supermarket. And maybe Phil and Sean, or Philippe and Sebastien as they preferred to be known, two hairdressers from Barnsley, whose salon abutted the end of our back lawn, leading our neighbour to observe from behind his newspaper that we had fairies at the bottom of our garden. You could say things like that in those days.

I used to imagine much more interesting dinner parties. Dinner parties with characters from history. Dinner parties where Napoleon would rub shoulders with Genghis Khan. Dinner parties where the Red Baron would discuss warfare with William the Conqueror. Not surprisingly for one so young, most of my imaginary dinner parties centred around combatants of one form or another.

Perhaps I should have a Parkie dinner party. The first guest would be easy: Muhammad Ali, the greatest, and one of the funniest men ever. Once asked by Michael Parkinson on a chat show whether it was an unwritten rule that boxers were expected to abstain from sex before a fight, he looked Parkinson in the eye and said "No Michael, it's *during* a fight".

I think Pope John Paul II would be a good choice as well. I can't help feeling that he and Muhammad Ali would hit it off. So who was the greatest? In any case, it's not every day that you have a pontiff -- and saint for that matter -- to say grace.

Every dinner party should have someone who is going to cause controversy. Someone who can be relied upon to evoke a reaction, to keep the conversation flowing. I reckon I have that base covered too. Probably not everyone's ideal choice of dinner guest but in the spirit of the game, I would pick Adolf Hitler. When it comes to Parkie dictators, we are spoiled for choice. Chairman Mao, Gen Franco and Deng Xiao Ping would be worth consideration for the tyranny seat at the table. Or we could have a sort of despot corner. But in the end, one dictator is more than enough and it's hard to trump Hitler. Besides I am trying to brush up my German.

We need someone to counterbalance the loudmouths - and although I think Hitler would be offended by the epithet, Muhammad Ali would take it as flattery. But I need a quieter man, a thinker, to balance Hitler's ranting. so I would suggest that a poet is in order. And I rather fancy John Betjeman. Well that's not what I meant, but as we both went to the same boarding school -- some years apart I should add -- one should assume nothing. I could put him next to Muhammad Ali. The Greatest used to pen the odd ditty.

We need an artist too so how about Salvador Dali. Okay, he's a fully paid-up wacko, with a dodgy moustache and he doesn't speak a word of English. Put him next to Hitler maybe?

Or we could have a corner of the table reserved for right wing politicos. That would give me the chance to bring Enoch Powell in. Sit him next to Hitler and they could foam at the mouth together. Maybe put Muhammad Ali on his left. Go on Enoch, give him the 'rivers of blood' speech. I hope you can take a punch.

Although Dali may be funny – honestly Sal, we're laughing *with* you – he is at best a titter rather than a guffaw. The party needs someone who will have us in stitches. And I have just the man – Terry Thomas. A comedian in his own right, but also a significant comic actor. His role in Those Magnificent Men in Their Flying Machines still cracks me up today.

One last seat and I'm torn between sport and movies – It should really be a sportsman for Muhammad to talk to. How about Basil D'Oliveira? Mmmmm....I'm not so sure Americans understand cricket. So I'll play safe and go for Vincent Price.

I'm a sucker for all the old horror films. I can't get over how many of them seem to have a formulaic titles along the lines of "xxxxxx of yyyyyy", where xxxxxx would be anything from a list including House, Theatre, Train, Castle or Labyrinth and yyyyyy would be chosen from another list including blood, death, ghosts, terror, zombies, madness or murder -- that sort of thing. Put together appropriately and you have "Theatre of Blood", "House of Ghosts" or pretty much any of the 1970s Hammer Horror output. I think they missed a trick though when they dropped "Bungalow of Zombies".

Okay so I'm biased, but Vincent Price is definitely on for dinner. Still, nobody who has seen Price's acting in The Abominable Dr Phibes can possibly fault my choice of him as a dinner guest. Besides, no roast dinner is complete without a ham.

This all leads me onto the subject of food. Soup is out of bounds for most Parkies -- nobody wants to be the first diner with a lap full of minestrone. The same goes for jelly -- short of nailing it to the spoon, there is no way that I could get jelly from plate to mouth successfully. I rather fancy the idea of serving kosher food if only to see Hitler's reaction. "It's chopped liver, fuhrer – just eat it and don't be such a baby". I should probably find out who's a veggie too. I can't help feeling that if God had meant us to eat only vegetables, he wouldn't have made animals quite so darn tasty. I'll have a quiet word with JP while we hand out the cheese footballs. He'll know. Or we could have tapas, just to make Salvador feel at home.

Of course the skill of good host is to steer conversation toward subjects of mutual interest and to try and head off any confrontation. Generally that rules out religion and politics. I'm sure the Pope can be relied upon not to talk shop but I'm less confident about the politicians. After all, when has a politician ever known when to shut up? So unless they can be relied upon to behave themselves, I shall have to silence half the guests. Probably best not to put Enoch and Adolf together. It will take more than a little persuasion to silence them. But then there's always duck tape.

In the end, the dinner party is a roaring success. It's hard to pick any highlights but Terry Thomas and Enoch Powell duetting a medley of old ska tunes together had Salvador's moustache twitching. And I have all those doodles and caricatures Dali drew on the napkins. It broke the ice. As did Betjeman who proved, after a couple of glasses of Scotch, that he'd never completely turned his back on the limerick's undoubted potential. And who would have guessed that Pope John Paul knew so many card tricks. Some of the conclaves of cardinals can drag a bit he said. Only Hitler let the side down, refusing to play charades any more when we failed to get his "I'm just a girl who can't say no" and sulking in a corner with his schnapps. In the end he made his excuses and left early, muttering something about annexing the Sudetenland. I wasn't really listening.

TEENAGE ANGST
Tuesday 27th September 2011

It's a tough gig being a teenager. When you are the source of all human knowledge, and let's face it who's ever met a teenager who didn't know it all, it's hard to put up with lesser beings. And lesser beings for the purposes of this discussion mean pretty much everybody else. And especially your parents.

As a teenager, your parents are, in large part, completely clueless. Worthless even. And there's nothing that depresses you more than the thought that you might actually be descended from them. You take one look at the bags under your mother's weary eyes or your father's expanding waistline and it's hard to believe that you are related to these embarrassing creatures. Hard to believe that you are obliged to tolerate these grotesques until you can earn enough money to move out and tell your parents where to stick their unconditional love malarkey. But you know what terrifies you most -- the thought that, however distant that timeframe, you too will somehow turn into these selfsame creatures, these paragons of self-neglect.

On the whole, as any self-respecting teenager will tell you, parents are best kept under wraps. Or better still, under house arrest. Parents are an embarrassment. Parkie parents doubly so. Whatever you do, don't let them have any contact with your friends. If necessary, lock your father in the tool shed and send your mother out to the supermarket, when expecting guests. I mean -- like -- doesn't your heart -- like -- sink, when your friends -- like -- come round and your parents meet them at the door. They probably want to frisk them for drugs. Or, worse still, they might actually simply want to be friendly. Shudder at the thought. And if you think that's bad, there is even the nightmare scenario -- that your parents might actually have something in common with your friends. Is there any situation most dispiriting than discovering that your friends actually like your parents. There is nothing your friends can say more calculated to cause distress than "I really like your mum/dad". I mean -- like -- what a terrible, insensitive thing to say. It's like when your father tells you "you are so like your mother".

And if you think that's bad, remember when your father danced in public. And everybody at the disco said "who is that loser?" And how Posy Rees had said "that's Alice's dad, isn't it Alice?" And how you seriously believed that if you prayed hard enough the ground would actually open and swallow you up.

Or when your mum came shopping with you for bras and knickers and stood aghast at the tiny, postage stamps of cloth that you seemed determined to wear in preference to the yards of whalebone and acres of tarpaulin suggested by her.

And why do your parents seem so determined to misinterpret your need to 'find yourself' or just 'need your own space' as a cry for help, best assuaged with a diet consisting of even more vegetables.

And why do your parents seem to think that three hours of Facebook each day is wasted. They're just jealous because they don't have any friends. And is there anything sadder than receiving a Facebook friend request from your mother or father. Er -- like -- no. Imagine if your friends noticed.

Parents. Like -- who needs them?

The Last Word

A CHANGE OF WORLDS
Friday 30th September 2011

In 1854, Chief Seattle of the Duwamish tribe, responded eloquently to governmental proposals that he and his tribe should be moved to a reservation. Years of warfare between the white and red man had come to the point where the tribes had nothing left.

He talked of the sky that had wept tears of compassion upon his people for centuries. He spoke of God, of the white man's God that folded strong protecting arms around the pale faces but had forsaken His red children. To him the red man was an ebbing, receding tide. And he spoke of death, the meaning of death and the difference between the white and red man's death.

Above all, he spoke of his ancestors, those who had gone before. For him and the Duwamish people, ancestors held sacred roles. The dead were not gone, but moved unseen around the living, to visit, guide and comfort. As he memorably put it "there is no death, only a change of worlds". When moved to a reservation distant from their own burial grounds, he feared his tribe would lose touch with their ancestors, and become a spiritually lost people.

Parkinson's was first acknowledged as a medical condition with the publication of "An Essay on the Shaking Palsy" in 1817 by James Parkinson. And in the nearly two centuries that have elapsed, we have found no cure. Indeed until forty years ago, there wasn't even a treatment. In those two centuries, millions, perhaps tens of millions, have lived with this condition. Their ghosts are all around us. They are our ancestors with this condition, stoic forefathers in the Parkinson tribe. And as surely as night follows day, we are one tribe. And even from their change of worlds our ancestors ask the same question -- when will we see a cure?

A year ago I attended the World Parkinson Congress in Glasgow. And I wrote a vision of the promised land, where we would see the cure. A year has gone by and I ask myself the same question our Parkinson's ancestors ask. Will it be tomorrow, next month, next year perhaps? Will it be in my lifetime?

The Parkinson's community is as focused as ever on this Holy Grail, this Nirvana. But a year has still gone by and our good words and intentions mean nothing to the tens of thousands with Parkinson's who have crossed over, called home by the silent throng of our tribal ancestors, and the many who will continue to do so. We can talk as much as we like about energy, about momentum and about enthusiasm but in the end it comes down to one thing. We want a cure. We want it now. There is nothing that would change our world more.

How many more moons must wax and wane? How many more winters must pass? How many more must walk in the footsteps of our tribal ancestors?

How many more tomorrows must become yesterdays before this thing is done?

SOME USEFUL ONLINE RESOURCES

CURE PARKINSON'S TRUST
www.cureparkinsons.org.uk

A modest sized patient-led charity with the clear intention of expediting a cure for Parkinson's. Funds research and always looking for volunteers.

PARKINSON'S UK
www.parkinsons.org.uk

The largest UK-based charity with a wealth of resources on its website and available by post or by download. Funds both research and care.

EUROPEAN PARKINSON'S DISEASE ASSOCIATION
www.rewritetomorrow.eu.com

Resources available, with a focus on symptoms symptom treatment. Very good book on nonmotor symptoms.

PARKINSON'S MOVEMENT
www.parkinsonsmovement.com

The new kid on the block. Website for patient advocacy, intended to help patients engage with their healthcare and future research agenda.

PARKINSON'S CREATIVE COLLECTIVE
www.parkinsonscreativecollective.org

A group of writers with Parkinson's have banded together to produce this pot pourri of meadow flowers.

WORLD PARKINSON CONGRESS
www.worldpdcongress.org

Important research and care Congress where patients and physicians mingle. A must if you are serious about this condition.